82

Family Adventures

Exploring the World with Children

gestalten

Table of Contents

ON THE ROAD TO FIND OUT

An Introduction by Austin Sailsbury

By the time we became parents, my wife Ashlyn and I had been living in Europe for more than four years. The arrival of our first child—like the arrival of all first children—marked the end of an era, a brief but golden chapter of life that we now realize we often took for granted. For years, we had lived simply, focused on our careers, and traveled every chance we could. We had spent summers in Italy, autumns in Paris, springtime in Spain. Looking back, it seems impossible that we ever had the ability to move so freely or travel so lightly. Back then, we didn't know what we didn't know.

And then, in August of 2016, Owen was born. That summer, we wondered if it was time to return home to the U. S. for good. Our future was hazy, bordering on opaque. But then we had an idea: what if we spent a year "abroad in America" to reconnect with family and friends, and get reacquainted with our homeland? Traveling was something we knew how to do, and—we had heard—newborns were easy companions. It sounded like the adventure of a lifetime. How hard could it be?

In October, as we flew west over the Atlantic, we still didn't know all the things we didn't know; about being parents, about life on the road with an infant, about what our marriage would look like with Owen in the mix. But it didn't take long to realize that our days as a pair of beach-lounging, paperback-reading, long-dinner-having wanderers were over. It seems obvious, of course: having a baby changes everything. But, like the other families in this book, we had to experience this new reality for ourselves.

Over the next 10 months, we visited 21 American states, driving more than 40,235 kilometers (25,000 miles) as we journeyed from Florida to California, and from Texas to Wisconsin. We lived out of two suitcases. We swam in two oceans. We stood in the shadows of great sequoias and at the top of the Blue Ridge Mountains. We voted. We went to Disney World. We found new friends and dug up old ones. We met oyster hunters in Charleston, a drag queen in Brooklyn, off-the-grid loners in the desert, and an ornery bear lumbering around our Airbnb near Yosemite. Most significantly, we watched our son bloom from a babbling baby into a quirky, stubborn, wonderful little boy who refused to fall asleep in the car unless we turned Chance the Rapper "up to 11." Frankly, we stumbled our way through that first year as parents, laughing and weeping in equal measure. We learned to let go of a lot during that first family adventure.

The Sailsbury family at home in Copenhagen, Denmark, in 2020. Below and next page: The family during their year traveling "abroad in America" in 2016/2017, pictured here visiting Muir Woods, the Grand Canyon, San Francisco, and Yosemite and Arches National Parks.

But we discovered a lot too. Bottom line, we survived a year on the road with a baby. Would we do it all again, knowing what we know now? Maybe not. But would we trade away that adventurous first year as a family, rediscovering America together? Not for all the sourdough in San Francisco.

"Taking risks, overcoming challenges, discovering beauty, and opening our minds and hearts. These are the things we hope for each time we pack our bags, load the car, or board a plane."

It was during this year of traveling, that I began wondering about how and why other parents continue to explore the world even after having children. The profiles in the following pages are a partial answer to that question. They offer a window into some of the inspiring ways that moms and dads are passing on a legacy of adventurous living to their kids. The stories in this book will take you from the deserts of Morocco to tropical Oahu, from the Amazon River to the Ionian Sea, and from the bustling markets of India to a soba-noodle party on a farm outside of Tokyo.

Some of these stories are about unique family vacations. Others focus on parents who want to instill a love of travel by exposing their children to life-changing, round-the-world journeys. Still others remind us how much we can learn from exploring the wonders hiding in plain sight—in our hometowns, our backyards, or that shady stand of pine trees we've driven past for years. But what all of these stories have in common, is their celebration of two of life's most challenging and rewarding endeavors: traveling and parenting.

These are real-life tales of moms and dads braving the unavoidable struggles of travel—flight delays, lost luggage, middle-of-nowhere engine breakdowns, and middle-of-everyone emotional meltdowns—to share new experiences with their kids. As all of these parents will tell you, traveling with kids is never easy. But the benefits can be invaluable. What could be more important than introducing our children to cultures where families, not so unlike our own, look and live and speak and eat differently than we do. What could be more useful than giving them the tools to deal with the challenges encountered on the road. Hannah Carpenter, whose family decamped to Italy for three months, sums up the complex beauty of family travel especially well. "Traveling with your family is incredible, and, at times, it's also incredibly awful. When you travel, you are still you, and your kids are still your kids. There's no magic travel dust that turns you all into the best versions of yourselves once you cross the Atlantic. You will fight and cry and fantasize about getting off one stop ahead of them on your train rides." But, she says, "Travel is a cure for so much of the bad that infects people. We know that the more we expose our kids to other cultures and places, the more likely they are to be more inclusive, open-minded, creative, and willing to take risks. We hope this experience has ignited a wanderlust in them, and a willingness to think more broadly about the world and their place in it."

Taking risks, overcoming challenges, discovering beauty, and opening our minds and hearts. These are the things we hope for each time we pack our bags, load the car, or board a plane. This is why we leave home and head into the unknown. No matter how old we are, each of us wants to be filled with awe and to feel fully alive. And we want to share these experiences with the people we love the most, so that these moments of wonder might live on for years to come.

AUSTIN SAILSBURY is an American writer whose work has been featured in numerous online and print publications, including Magnolia Journal, Kinfolk Magazine, *and* Ark Journal. *He is also the author of three books about travel and lifestyle. He lives with his family in Copenhagen.*

Baby on Board: A European Surfing Safari

BORDEAUX, HOSSEGOR, BIARRITZ, SAN SEBASTIÁN, MUNDAKA, NAZARÉ, ERICEIRA, SAGRES (FRANCE, SPAIN, AND PORTUGAL)

KATJANA FRISCH AND TOBIAS LEYENDECKER, KOA (2 MONTHS)

A pair of surfer parents introduces their newborn son to the joys of sea, sand, and sun along the Atlantic coast.

"The only plan was to begin the trip from our home in Munich, head toward the Atlantic Ocean and go surfing," says photographer Katjana Frisch. This was to be a surf trip similar to many she had previously undertaken with her partner, Tobias Leyendecker, only this time the couple would have their newborn son tagging along for the ride. "As a new mom and dad, we wanted to have the time and opportunity to get to know our baby in a special atmosphere—not in the everyday routine but out in nature and close to the ocean," Katjana says. The couple first came up with the idea of a post-birth Atlantic surfing adventure during Katjana's pregnancy. They were staying on the Hawaiian island of Oahu at the time, where Tobias was utilizing his skills as a carpenter to build a surf shop. "We just wanted to keep on traveling with our baby," says Katjana. So, in November 2019, when baby Koa was only two months old, the family set off on an overland European tour toward the sea, the sun, and the surf.

Although they had no strict itinerary, Katjana and Tobias did have the perfect vehicle for their trip: a repurposed Mercedes-Benz Sprinter named *Bumble Bee,* which Tobias had equipped with everything they might need. Once the family hit the road, they mapped out a wave-hunting expedition that would take them from Germany to the French surfing paradises of Bordeaux,

Informação Local
Rota Sul
MIRADOURO
FURNAS
PRAIA PESCADORES
PORTO PESCA
IGREJA S^to ANTONIO
CASA DA CULTURA
BRIGADA FISCAL
DELEGAÇÃO MARITIMA
Navegue com Informação
Junta de Freguesia da Ericeira

In November 2019, when baby Koa was only two months old, the family set off on an overland European tour toward the sea, the sun, and the surf. “The only plan was to head toward the Atlantic Ocean and go surfing,” says photographer Katjana Frisch.

The family's epic surfing adventure took them to Bordeaux, Hossegor, and Biarritz, France; then to San Sebastián and Mundaka, Spain; and, finally, to Nazaré, Ericeira, and Sagres, in Portugal.

During the journey, Katjana and Tobias met other families with a shared love and respect for the natural world. Those encounters emboldened them in their own parenting ethos and their commitment to "showing our child what's really important in life."

WAVEGLIDERS
WAVEGLIDERS
SURF SHOP
Deus
EX MACHINA
WAVEGLIDERS
SURFING

"As a new mom and dad, we wanted to have the time and opportunity to get to know our baby in a special atmosphere—not in the everyday routine but out in nature and close to the ocean."

Hossegor, and Biarritz; then to the Spanish sands of San Sebastián and Mundaka; and, finally, to the stunning Portuguese beaches of Nazaré, Ericeira, and Sagres. "We decided on destinations where we would feel safe and where we already had friends," Katjana says.

Life on the road with a newborn brought about its own specific challenges for the family. No longer could Tobias and Katjana travel vast, uninterrupted distances overland to catch the perfect weather formations for surfing. "For me, it mattered most that the baby wouldn't have to sit too long in his car seat," Katjana explains, "so this trip had a new routine: short distances between stops, and a lot of breaks for breastfeeding, walking in the fresh air, and playing."

While Katjana found caring for Koa on the trip relatively straightforward—"they don't need a lot at the beginning"—her first time back on a surfboard after giving birth was a different story. "The first few times I got in the water with my post-pregnancy body, I was frustrated and disappointed," she says. "Paddling was difficult, and other maneuvers were just out of the question." But as often happens on adventures like these, a chance meeting changed her entire perspective. In Portugal, near the couple's final surf destination of Sagres, Katjana met an older man, a surfboard shaper, to whom she vented her frustrations. Furrowing his brow in thought, he told her: "Don't go surfing, go fishing; when a wave is coming for you, take it. If not, just watch for fish in the ocean." After quite literally taking that advice on board, Katjana says, "I was finally surfing again."

In the cave-like atmosphere of their bus, Katjana and Tobias witnessed many of Koa's first milestones: his first true smiles, the first time he clutched a toy, his first kicks and coos. "Our little boy learned and grew so much on the road," Katjana enthuses. "He changed from a little helpless newborn into a wild baby boy who started to recognize his surroundings more and more." Since the trip took place over the December holiday period, the couple introduced Koa to Christmas in an unconventional way, while they were staying in a remote, deserted bay surrounded by boulders and giant sea swells. "We had found an old Algarve tree lying on the ground, and, deciding it would make a very special Christmas tree, Tobi lashed it to the back of the bus," Katjana says. "I decorated the tree with some pine cones and spray-painted it gold. Koa was happy about the new games in the bus. It was a peaceful Christmas. We ate fish burgers, and the smell hung around for days afterward, reminding us of the good time we had."

This intimate, one-of-a-kind journey was a learning experience for the entire family, and Katjana is quick to highlight the benefits of this style of travel. "Being in buses, it's easy to experience other concepts of family life," she says. "People are very open to showing their own reality, it doesn't take place behind closed doors." On the beaches and in the many surf towns they visited, Katjana and Tobias met a number of families who had a shared love and respect for the natural world. Those encounters emboldened them in their own parenting ethos and their commitment to "showing our children what's really important in life, allowing them to dream, and helping them to find their passions." In the end, their first travel adventure with Koa was a powerful reminder of all they have to offer their son. "Parents who give up their lives and their identities for their kids," Katjana muses, "what do they have left to give them?"

Explore More

SURFING IN EUROPE?
Believe it or not, some of the best waves in the world are found in Europe, from Scotland to Morocco. And although surfing had been tried in the 19th century, it took off in Europe in the 1950s and 1960s.

FRANCE
There are quality surf spots to be found all along France's Atlantic coast, with elegant Biarritz as the favorite. Look for mellow waves in summer and big, competition-size waves in the autumn and winter.

SPAIN
San Sebastián, in the Basque region of Spain, is the ideal base for a surfing vacation. In addition to great breaks, the region offers many great things for families to see, do, and—most importantly—to eat.

PORTUGAL
Portugal is much loved by travelers for its sunshine, great food, beautiful towns, and friendly locals. Surfers love the breaks all along the coast, from Algarve in the south all the way north to Porto.

THE BEST OF THE REST
Believe it or not, you can surf in England, Ireland, Scotland, and in Klitmøller, Denmark–known locally as "cold Hawaii." Or, bring a board to The Eisbach Wave, a popular river wave in Munich's English Garden.

In the cave-like atmosphere of their bus, Katjana and Tobias witnessed many of Koa's first milestones: his first true smiles, the first time he clutched a toy, his first kicks and coos.

TRAVEL TIPS: ZERO TO TWO

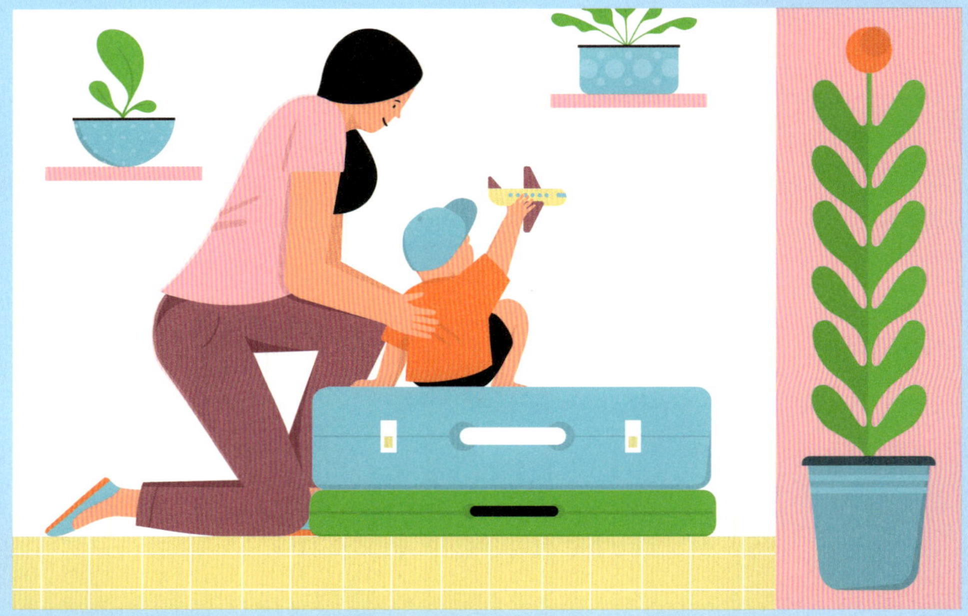

There will always be naysayers when it comes to traveling with very young children. You're likely to hear comments such as, "They won't remember it," or, "It's too much work." But are memories the only justification for travel? And how much work is too much? Yes, at this age, children need near-constant care, and yes, the planning and in-transit phases may be more complicated, but seeing a child's enjoyment in experiencing new things for the first time—even though they might not remember it—cancels out any need to justify traveling with them. As with any trip, it's the little moments that matter.

Choosing a Destination

Exploring within your own borders or continent is a simple and cost-effective option for a trip with children aged zero to two. Aim for a relatively stress-free jaunt, or even a multi-stop road trip that can be undertaken at any pace.

Picturesque and peaceful destinations such as beaches, mountain ranges, or heritage towns are good options—locations where both children and parents can get a good amount of rest on their own schedule. If traveling in summer, ensure your destination won't be excessively hot, as heat-related sicknesses can be a concern for young children.

How to Get There

Long-haul flights can be tricky with children in this age group, but with the right preparation, they are manageable. Bringing two bags into the cabin—a smaller one you can take with you to the bathroom and a bigger one from which to restock it—can make all the difference.

On booking, ask what your airline offers in the way of bassinets for children under two—amenities differ between airlines. When it comes to check-in, make sure you're all sitting together, either at the front of the seating sections for the extra room, or near a window so you can lean into it with your child.

You'll also want to disinfect everything with a sanitary wipe as soon as you sit down.

Checklist (On the Plane)

- Passport (if traveling internationally)
- Travel insurance
- Breast milk or formula (in Europe and the United States, the standard 100-milliliter policy does not apply to reasonable quantities of such liquids)
- Baby food (no, you will most likely not be able to feed your baby from the airplane's, or even airport, food options. But don't hesitate to ask the cabin crew for help to warm it up, use cutlery, etc.)
- Diapers (roughly one per hour of flight time, and allow for delays)
- Diaper cream
- Changing pad
- Baby wipes
- Sanitary wipes (to clean your seating area)
- Plastic bags (to dispose of the trash you will be generating, collect things quickly, or carry whatever you might buy along the way)
- Prescription medications, and baby acetaminophen or ibuprofen (if suitable for age)
- Digital thermometer
- Snacks
- Blankets (for use while breastfeeding, wrapping babies, and covering the floor of an improvised play area)
- Changes of clothes (for both parents and children)
- Several toys (if your child is old enough, wrap them up cleverly in advance so unwrapping them can become a game in itself)
- A tablet and headphones (depending on the age of the child)

Where to Sleep

Airbnb states: "Infants (children under two years old) aren't counted as guests when you're booking a reservation and don't incur any extra costs." Hotels, however, depending on location and type, do sometimes charge for infants, so check this when booking. During that process, also check that the accommodations will provide something suitable for young children to sleep in, and whether there's a restaurant on site. If there is, ask if it has highchairs—you might end up eating there more than you think. True family-friendly hotels might even offer daycare and babysitting services, so parents can finally make it out for that meal and movie.

Where to Eat

There is an open secret among parents with young children: eat early. Obviously, this ensures bedtimes can be met, but if you're eating at a restaurant, it also means that there's a good chance the venue will be nearly empty, or filled with busy families like your own, so there's no need to fear interrupting the peaceful meals of fellow patrons. When it comes to family-friendly restaurants, a quick location-specific internet search will give you a range of options, some of which may even have play areas for toddlers—a relaxing alternative to the timeless game of running out the door.

How to Move Around

Strollers and public transport can be a stressful combination, especially if you're traveling solo as a parent. But braving a bus or train is often a necessary part of moving around a city with an infant or toddler. Beyond the benefit of being a place for travel-weary children to sleep, a stroller provides storage room for the vital equipment busy parents need, and the extra space is particularly helpful if you plan to be out all day. If you are solo parenting and need help getting on or off public transport, don't be afraid to ask someone to assist you.

Unexpected Twists

It is not uncommon for children in this age range to develop fevers. A child might become hotter than usual, have red cheeks, and they may behave differently, becoming grumpy or unusually sensitive.

Keep a digital thermometer on hand when you travel so you can check their temperature yourself, and it's always a good idea to have temperature-alleviating baby acetaminophen or ibuprofen as a permanent component of your baby bag, even if only for real emergencies. In such situations, knowing you have travel health insurance that will cover your baby can be a huge relief, so ensure you get this before you leave.

Hack

When you're stuck on a long-haul plane or train ride, there may well be moments when your child just won't stop crying. In times like these, don't panic. The problem can usually be solved with the simple introduction of a toy—the brighter, chewier, and squishier the better.

For the best results, bring along a new, unseen toy, or one that you've hidden away for a while that your child won't recognize—the sheer novelty should be enough to staunch the tears. For the sake of your fellow confined passengers, do not include any sound-making toys in your selection, as they could be a further irritation.

A Life-Changing Season of Old World Wandering

ITALY

HANNAH AND HEATH CARPENTER, TRISTIN (17), SILAS (13), ENID (11), AND TOM (8)

A family decamps from Arkansas to Italy for three months of immersive education and once-in-a-lifetime adventures.

"It was my husband Heath's dream to take our family of six to Europe for three months," Hannah Carpenter recalls, "which sounded like a nightmare to me: I'm more introverted than not, terrified of flying, I get motion sickness, and I was dreading the process of constantly moving our kids from place to place. So, as you can imagine, I'm a real joy as a travel companion." But, now, looking back on her family's European adventure, Hannah says, "I couldn't be happier to admit I was wrong. I can honestly say those were three of the best months of my life."

The Carpenter family lives in central Arkansas, where Heath is a university professor and Hannah works as an illustrator and small business owner. In early 2019, the family had the opportunity to decamp from the Ozarks to Florence to be part of a study abroad program connected to Heath's job. Coincidentally, both Heath and Hannah had attended the same program in Italy nearly two decades earlier. "When we studied abroad," Hannah remembers, "we slept in train stations, on the floor of boats, and in hostels of various repute, which enabled us to see a lot of Europe on a student budget. Between the two of us, we hit most of Italy and parts of Austria, Germany, the Czech Republic, Denmark, Holland, Switzerland, France, and the United Kingdom."

"Michelangelo used to play cards over here, Machiavelli partied over there, and Da Vinci used to sketch right over here. It sounds absurd to say these kinds of things, but in Tuscany, it happens all the time. Only in Italy!"

Although there would never be a "perfect" time to transplant their entire family abroad for three months, Hannah and Heath felt this was a can't-miss moment. "In another year, Tristin would be off to college," Hannah says, "and soon she'd have her own foreign adventures to plan, so we knew this was going to be the one time all six of us would have together abroad." In Italy, Heath and Hannah planned to return to the sites of some of their favorite travel memories. Older, wiser, and now with four kids in tow, the couple didn't know exactly what to expect, but they knew it would be an entirely different kind of adventure the second time around.

For the next 90 days, the family's base was a sixteenth-century villa located in the hills just outside of Florence—shared with 30 American college students from Heath's university program. "It was the exact same villa we stayed in as students," Hannah says. "We had a couple of acres to ourselves, with views of olive groves, umbrella pines, cypress trees, and broad Tuscan valleys. On clear days, you could see the Duomo in Florence." Because the university employed two local women to cook all the meals, the family was able to enjoy homemade Tuscan food every single day, an experience Hannah describes as a culinary "dream." As for their living arrangements, things were "a smidge more dicey." All four Carpenter kids shared one room with a small, en suite bathroom. "It's worth noting," Hannah says, "that one of those kids was a teenage girl, so Tristin certainly deserves the award for most patient Carpenter during our time at the villa."

Most evenings, after dinner, the family took long, meandering walks through the surrounding countryside. "The Italians have this phrase," Hannah explains, *"una passeggiata,* which means an aimless walk or stroll that you take just for the pleasure of it, and our nightly *passeggiata* became one of our favorite things to do together."

When not "at home" in Florence, Hannah and the kids joined Heath and his students as they toured the sights of the city and the surrounding regions. The group's journeys included visits to Rome, Venice, Naples, and Pompei, the mountain village of Campagna, the coastal towns of Sorrento and Paestum, and a brief ski trip

“We know that the more we expose our kids to other cultures and places, the more likely they are to be more inclusive, open-minded, and willing to take risks,” says Hannah Carpenter. “We hope this experience has ignited a sense of wanderlust in them.”

"When I look back, I get emotional," says Hannah Carpenter. "Though we felt a bit like the Griswolds from *National Lampoon's European Vacation* at times, the trip bonded us in ways that are hard to translate into words."

"It was my husband's dream to take our family of six to Europe for three months, which sounded like a nightmare to me. I couldn't be happier to admit I was wrong. I can honestly say those were three of the best months of my life."

in a village called Abetone. The highlight among highlights for the Carpenters was their coast-to-coast trip across Sicily. "Sicily is old-world Italy," Hannah says, "It's glamorous and rustic, exotic and local all in one: Roman ruins, medieval customs, folk dancing in the street, and, of course, the food. The unspoiled landscapes and mountains are like a dreamscape of plant life straight out of a Dr. Seuss book."

Despite the thrill of these adventures, many days were completely exhausting. "When we were with the group, it was non-stop, 20,000-step days," Hannah recalls. "We have a running joke about how many times Tommy would fall asleep at some bustling Italian restaurant before his food arrived. He'd wake up in a fit of wide-eyed confusion not knowing if he was in Arkansas or Austria, and Heath would speak to him slowly, as if he had been in a coma for a month: "Tommy, you've been asleep; we're in Rome now; you ordered ravioli."

After Italy, the Carpenters took one month to travel around Europe alone as a family, to London, Oxford, Paris, and Bad Gastein, in Austria. Looking back, Heath and Hannah view the whirlwind of activity and immersive learning as a "mosaic of micro-experiences" that came together to profoundly impact the entire family. "Our kids experienced so many 'firsts,'" says Hannah. "Their first overnight flight, first tram ride, first overnight train and boat trips. For Enid and Tommy, it was their first time to swim in the sea, with the Italian Alps as a backdrop! By the end of three months, the kids were seasoned pros—they were unfazed by navigating London, Florence, Paris, wherever. That growth was really special to watch."

From their own past experiences traveling in Europe, the Carpenters believe that their kids' worldviews were undoubtedly expanded during their time abroad. "We know that the more we expose them to other cultures and places, the more likely they are to be more inclusive, open-minded, creative, and willing to take risks," Hannah says. "We hope this experience has ignited a sense of wanderlust in them, and a willingness to think more broadly about the world and their place in it."

Back home in Arkansas, Hannah says her family regularly has "remember when..." conversations that inevitably result in a snowball of storytelling and laughter around the kitchen table. *Remember the impromptu dance party in Palermo. Remember the picnic under the Eiffel Tower. Remember the protests in Paris. Remember when mom had a panic attack riding the ski lift to the top of the mountain.*

"When I look back, I get emotional," Hannah says. "I will never again have that time with our family just as it was. Though we felt a bit like the Griswolds from *National Lampoon's European Vacation* at times, the trip bonded us in ways that are hard to translate into words; it's a mixture of sadness for a time gone and thankfulness mixed with joy that we will always have this shared experience to remember."

For Hannah and Heath Carpenter, investing in family experiences of all shapes and sizes is rewarding in ways it's hard to articulate. "If you can travel, I highly encourage it," Hannah says. "Travel is a cure for so much of the bad that infects people, but the life you share as a family at home is just as significant. We know that with Heath's job, we were in a really unique position to travel the way we did. But, if you can't travel the world, your family can still grow and live a full life, and you aren't robbing your kids of anything. You don't have to travel to Europe to explore the beauty and diversity of the world. There are little bits of paradise all around us that we can introduce to our kids today. Then, one day, they'll be able to set off on life-changing adventures of their own because of the love and confidence you instill in them."

Explore More

CUSTOMIZE YOUR EXPERIENCE

Italy is a big country, with 60 million people and 301,340 square kilometers (116,348 square miles) to explore (stretching 1,500 kilometers [932 miles] from Sicily to Milan!). So, likely, you won't be able to experience it all in one trip.

ADVENTURE ESSENTIALS

Late spring or early fall is the best time to visit Italy. For moving around Italy with kids, skip the trains and rent a car, which is cheaper and will allow for much more flexibility and spontaneity.

WHERE TO GO

The best Italian cities for history and culture are, naturally, Rome, Florence, and Venice. For iconic Italian beach culture, try Cinque Terre, the Amalfi Coast, and rugged Puglia in the south.

STAY ON NONNA'S FARM

For a truly authentic Italian experience, stay at an agriturismo. Found throughout the country, these working farms offer so much that a hotel can't (including home-cooked meals and hands-on learning).

LIVIN' "LA DOLCE VITA"

For the most quintessential Italian experience possible, find a spot at any outdoor cafe, order an espresso or two, and spend some time soaking up the sun while watching the parade of life buzz all around.

"The Italians have this phrase," Hannah Carpenter explains, "*una passeggiata,* which means an aimless walk or stroll that you take just for the pleasure of it, and our nightly *passeggiata* became one of our favorite things to do together."

On the Go in Copenhagen: A Father-Son Duo Explore Their Hometown

COPENHAGEN, DENMARK

VIRGIL NICHOLAS AND VINNY (2)

An entrepreneurial dad balances career and fatherhood by including his young son in the way he works and networks.

Welcoming a baby into a family disrupts much more than his or her parents' sleep. It can feel like a tsunami of change that affects every aspect of daily life, forcing new moms and dads to adjust the ways in which they socialize and work. For Virgil Nicholas, a Copenhagen-based fashion consultant and entrepreneur, becoming a father in 2018 meant a lot of change, yes, but it also meant an opportunity to include his young son, Vincent-Laurent (also known as Vinny), in the way he works, networks, and engages with the exciting world of Danish design and Scandinavian fashion.

Along with launching his own footwear brand, Vinny's, in 2019, Virgil Nicholas has spent the last decade working as a fashion consultant for menswear brands such as GANT, NN07, Tommy Hilfiger, and Les Deux. Whether directing photoshoots, helping to launch a new flagship store, or creating original social media content, Virgil's work is, by nature, highly dynamic and intensely social. It is work that takes him to every corner of the city, from the offices of top menswear designers to VIP after-parties during Copenhagen Fashion Week. A self-described "people person" with a warm smile and an infectious laugh, Virgil makes personal, authentic connections wherever he goes. And, it would seem, little Vinny is cut from the same social cloth. "Less than two weeks after he was born, Vinny's mom and I took him with

As they've explored Copenhagen extensively over the years, Virgil and Vinny have developed a kind of rhythm that takes them back to a few favorite places around the city. In the bustling center of Copenhagen, the pair has several spots that they frequent.

Virgil and Vinny Nicholas have a shared and ever-growing love for the city and people of Copenhagen. “One thing is for sure: both of us are explorers to the core,” says Virgil. “For us, any full day spent inside is a day wasted.”

"Since Vinny was born, I've found myself exploring Copenhagen more than ever before, and in some fun new ways. This is a city where I can bring my son along with me anywhere; I never feel that he is unwelcome."

us to a Fashion Week brunch and he has been coming along with us to every Fashion Week since," says Virgil with a smile. "He's so positive and open-minded, and he's an amazing networker—seriously, you should see this little guy work a room."

After Virgil's girlfriend AK went back to work in 2019, Vinny had to wait about nine months for placement in the local kindergarten. During this time, Virgil decided he would bring his son along for whatever work-related events he had on his calendar. Vinny's naturally warm disposition and lack of fear around strangers allowed the pair to move freely about town on an almost daily basis, meeting up for coffee with friends and colleagues, exploring Copenhagen's historic center, and attending client meetings. "Since Vinny was born, I've found myself exploring Copenhagen more than ever before, and in some really fun new ways," Virgil says. "The truth is, this is a city where I can bring my son along with me pretty much anywhere; I never feel that he is unwelcome."

As they've explored Copenhagen extensively over the past two years, Virgil and Vinny have developed a kind of rhythm that regularly takes them back to a few favorite places around the city. "If we want to stick close to home, we almost always head to the beach near our apartment," Virgil says. "Winter or summer, Vinny loves everything about the waterfront: the sights, sounds, and smell of it all." Not far away, in the bustling center of Copenhagen, the pair has several spots that they frequent. "Typically, we load up the stroller, hop onto the harbor bus, and head to one of the city's amazing parks, where Vinny can climb, slide, play with other kids, and splash in puddles for hours." After playtime, the guys will usually head to a favorite bakery or cafe for a midday pick-me-up. More often than not, the pair will end up at The Union Kitchen, a beloved local hotspot renowned for its weekend brunch. "Aside from serving the best truffle fries in town—which are Vinny's favorite food in the world—this is a place we love coming back to time and again," Virgil says. "Vinny feels at home here; he enjoys interacting with the staff, meeting up with my friends, and then, inevitably, he'll fall asleep for a while and give me a chance to socialize with some adults."

Now that he is two years old, Vinny attends a local kindergarten while his mom and dad are working. Naturally, this means Virgil brings his sidekick along for fewer weekday meetings and work events than he used to. But it doesn't mean that this father and son team has given up their shared love of exploring the city together. "We definitely still make time for adventures," Virgil says. "Often, when I pick Vinny up from daycare, we head straight to the beach, take off our shoes, and run around until he's basically exhausted." Weekends, too, have a new special quality. "That's when we have more time to be together; AK and I love to let Vinny be a part of the decision about what we're going to do as a family." Whether it's a trip to the beach after school or a spontaneous weekend outing to one of Copenhagen's colorful neighborhoods, Virgil and Vinny Nicholas have an ever-growing love for the city and people of Copenhagen. "One thing is for sure: both of us are explorers to the core," says Virgil. "For us, any full day spent inside is a day wasted."

Explore More

WONDERFUL COPENHAGEN
Copenhagen—like the other Nordic capitals—is a city that's especially friendly to families: it's clean, well-organized, safe, and has lots of green spaces and amazing playgrounds to explore.

HANDS-ON LEARNING
Copenhagen's zoo is world class, with stunning architecture, creative playgrounds, and gourmet food trucks. North of town, the Experimentarium provides a full day's worth of science fun for all ages.

ICONIC FUN SINCE 1843
Hosting nearly five million visitors a year, Tivoli Gardens is the best-known attraction in town and its reputation as one of the world's most beautiful amusement parks is well deserved.

TAKE TO THE SEA
Copenhagen has an extensive waterfront, lovely beaches, and a quaint canal system. Services like GoBoat, Hey Captain, and Netto Boats make it easy for visitors and locals alike to get out on the water.

LIKE RIDING A BIKE
For an authentic Copenhagen experience, rent or borrow some bikes, strap in the kids, throw on your helmets, and join the locals as they cruise along the city's elaborate network of bike lanes.

Discover Your Own City as a Tourist

By Katharina Marisa Katz

When my daughter Pauline was nine months old, we moved from Berlin back to my old home in Hamburg. For me, it was a real adventure to get to know this city that was so familiar to me, through a child's eyes.

"Before your first child, you might have judged a café by its cakes or chic interiors; having a baby makes changing tables, cozy quiet corners, and decaffeinated coffee a reason to visit."

So much changes with a child. Above all, you have completely new needs—and these seem to change every week, with every little step in development. But if you're navigating a city with a child, it's always useful to find the most beautiful walking routes that can be easily reached with a stroller. In Hamburg, the banks of the Außenalster lake have wonderful long paths with numerous small cafés for the necessary intake of caffeine after a busy night. Before your first child, you might have judged a café by its cakes or chic interiors; having a baby makes changing tables, cozy quiet corners, and decaffeinated coffee a reason to visit.

After a few months, we knew every path that an insecure little runner could try out safely and still find enough motivation to continue. Afternoons were planned around playgrounds, ice-cream parlors, and park visits. Since Pauline learned to walk in the fall, we faced the additional challenge of finding a place that was reasonably dry. So, we spent the fall and half of the winter in the Zoological Museum—lots of animals, a defined, safe room, and a flat floor: perfect conditions! Now Pauline can say that her first racetrack led from the seal to the blue whale.

Once your child can walk properly, the family becomes more mobile and you can start to conquer the city together. To really get to know the heart of a city, find a handful of favorite places—places that touch you, and where you immediately feel at home. Like many cities, Hamburg is most beautiful in summer. But something that Hamburg has over other cities is water—lots of water. Whether by the Elbe or the Alster rivers, there is nothing more beautiful than watching large ships on their way to distant countries with your feet in the sand. The best place for that is on the Elbe beach: just opposite the large harbor is a small beach hut, the Strandperle, where you can get ice cream and cold drinks in summer, the children can dig in the sand, and at regular intervals you can hear the deep thud of a cargo ship for added wanderlust.

With a child by your side, you get to know a city in a different way. It smells different, tastes different, and often sounds completely different. Children discover things that we adults don't notice. My daughter is thrilled about every squirrel that jumps in our way and detects every duck in a pond from a great distance. If the baker on the other side of the street has fresh cinnamon buns, she develops a real super nose. So we like to make ourselves comfortable in one of the many small cafés in Eimsbüttel with milk foam for Pauline and a cappuccino for me, creating small, cozy oases outside our own four walls. The corner around the Grindelhof is especially great for children: At Luicella's, you can try the best ice cream in town in summer and in the Salon Wechsel Dich you can enjoy waffles with warm plum compote in winter. Frau Büchert is directly opposite, an excellent small bookstore that offers a wonderful selection of children's books. Plus, the university area with its large fountain, small garden, and plenty of space for running or riding a scooter is nearby.

"Once your child can walk properly, the family becomes more mobile and you can start to conquer the city together. To really get to know the heart of a city, find a handful of favorite places—places that touch you, and where you immediately feel at home."

Hamburg is also ideal for bike tours—simply put your little explorer in the child seat and the adventure can begin. We usually just ride off into the blue and see where we end up—as long as we have a soccer ball and some bread to feed the ducks, Pauline likes it everywhere. If you want to go a little further afield, the Niendorf enclosure is a great destination, deer and horses included. On our bike trips we have already found some special places where few tourists or not too many other people go—places that only belong to us, at least at certain moments of the day. One of these is the small square on the edge of the Außenalster lake. We like to go there when half the city is still sleeping and it's shrouded in early-morning fog. If you are very quiet, you can spot sleepy ducks with their beaks hidden in their feathers, sneak up close and peacefully marvel at them.

When traveling, you are so often on the lookout for the great adventure, the very special memory, and with children these are sometimes waiting right outside the front door. Just let yourself be led by their ideas, their needs, and their sneaky little noses—you will be surprised by what you discover!

"When traveling, you are so often on the lookout for the great adventure, the very special memory, and with children these are sometimes waiting right outside the front door."

KATHARINA MARISA KATZ is a journalist, author, and creative consultant for media agencies, publishing houses and clients such as Sony Music, IKEA, Netflix, and Kitchen Stories. Since publishing her first book Einfach Machen—Der Guide für Gründerinnen (Make it Simple—The Guide for Female Founders) *in 2018, she has become a regular guest on panels and workshops devoted to launching creative ideas from scratch and founding a girlboss business.*

From Such Great Heights: Seeing the World from a New Perspective

CORSICA, FRANCE

SOPHIA AND CHRISTIAN METZLER-JÄGER, CLARA (2.5)

A family of climbing enthusiasts journeys to rugged Corsica and introduces their toddler to bouldering beside the sea.

From a young age, Sophia Metzler-Jäger inherited a desire to explore the world and its many natural wonders. "I was raised by my grandparents, and we traveled somewhere interesting nearly every school holiday; I've seen a lot of the world because of them." Later, she says, "My husband Christian and I fell in love with traveling so that we could climb in new places; now, rock-climbing holidays have just become part of who we are."

Their preferred method of rock climbing is called bouldering, a style of navigating up and around medium-sized rock formations (usually less than six meters [20 feet] tall) without a harness or safety ropes. But the couple's passion for climbing is about much more than the thrill of conquest. "Climbing is one of those unique experiences that helps you connect with a place on a much deeper level," Sophia says. "Touching the landscape creates memories of a place that are lasting and meaningful. So when Clara was born, we knew we wanted to share this passion with her—take her out into the world with us so that she could make deep connections of her own."

When not traveling the world in a camper van, Sophia and her family live in a small town in the mountainous Allgäu region in Germany. With her popular blog *Maybe You Like,* Sophia shares inspirational travel stories that she hopes will empower parents

"Climbing is one of those unique experiences that helps you connect with a place on a much deeper level," says Sophia Metzler-Jäger. "Touching the landscape creates memories of a place that are lasting and meaningful."

Corsica became a milestone in Clara's journey to becoming an independent explorer. "This was the first trip where she made her own choices and asked to see things that interested her," Sophia says.

"People are surprised that we can take such adventurous vacations with her, let alone manage to go climbing. But she loves it. And we're thrilled that we can share this passion as a family."

to continue traveling even after they have children. "My goal is to inspire people to go outside and bring their little ones along," she says. In the summer of 2019, the family decided to put this philosophy into practice by taking their young daughter to Corsica for her first climbing holiday.

Although only the fourth largest island in the Mediterranean, the French island of Corsica is the most mountainous. Many of its rugged beaches are dotted with large megalithic boulders, making it an ideal destination for adventurers who want to mix rock climbing with some time relaxing in the sand. "I got so excited looking at pictures of the rough coastlines and thinking about the wild river walks and hikes," Sophia recalls, "so we packed up our camper van and headed south."

After taking the ferry over from Italy, the family's Corsican journey started in Bastia, a centuries-old port town known for the historic church of Saint-Jean-Baptiste and a captivating citadel built during Genoese rule in the fourteenth century. Bastia has one of the main concentrations of non-granite climbing on the island and is home to dozens of gorgeous climbing sites. Next, they drove to Punta di Spanu, a protected natural maritime site with numerous scenic locations for bouldering near the water, before heading down the coast to Ota for some freestyle climbing in the area's beautiful red-granite cliffs. "Bouldering really offered us nice perspectives of each of the places we visited," Sophia explains. "Christian and I would take turns climbing and watching Clara so that everyone was able to enjoy the full experience." While their itinerary was open-ended, they took care to ensure Clara stayed happy. "We timed lots of naps for when we were driving from A to B," Sophia says, "and we've found that her mood can usually be swayed with snacks, stickers, or some fun children's music."

The family's adventure in Corsica became a milestone in Clara's journey to becoming an independent explorer. "This was the first trip where she made her own choices and asked to see things that interested her," Sophia says. "It was also the first time she went on her own little adventures and then talked about them later." Sophia's advice for families new to traveling with kids is simple: "Just try it, and don't stop doing what you love; take things slowly and see how your kids respond to different activities." She also recommends starting small, "a quick stay in a van, a tent, an Airbnb or even a hotel—whatever works within your comfort level."

Sophia is already looking forward to future climbing trips as a family. "We're expecting another baby soon, and I can't wait until we're all able to climb and explore together," she says. Both she and Christian hope their climbing expeditions will create lasting memories for their family and inspire other parents to share their passions—whatever they may be—with their own children, while exploring the world together.

Explore More

CORSICA: A BRIEF HISTORY

Once a Roman colony, for centuries Corsica was ruled by Italy. In 1768, the island was sold to France. A year later, on August 15, 1769, Napoleon Bonaparte was born in Corsica, in the town of Ajaccio.

TAKE A HIKE

The island is the fourth largest (and most mountainous) in the Mediterranean sea, with Monte Cinto as its highest peak (at 2,706 meters [8,878 feet] above sea level) and 1,000 kilometers (620 miles) of coastline.

TOO GOOD TO EXPORT

Corsica's climate is perfect for making wine and the island's viticultural history goes back millennia. But, enjoy it while you're there because most of the wine made on Corsica, stays on Corsica.

GO RIVER SWIMMING

There are more than 40 wild swimming spots scattered around Corsica, though kid-friendly access to these inland rivers, natural pools, and waterfalls varies. Consult a local before setting off.

NICE TO KNOW

Many islanders speak *u corsu* (along with French), a native language similar to Italian. Also, there are a number of picturesque Genoese bridges scattered around the island—keep your eyes open for those.

Still as Enchanting as Ever: Rediscovering "La Dolce Vita" in Italy

ROME, PUGLIA, AND THE AMALFI COAST (ITALY)

IRENE DE KLERK WOLTERS AND ARJAN KES, BEAU (14) AND PEPIJN (9)

As a girl, Irene de Klerk Wolters spent her summers in Italy; now she is introducing the sweet life to her own kids.

"I can still see my mom walking through the outdoor markets in the towns around Lake Garda, wearing the new summer clothes and handmade leather shoes she had just bought," says artist Irene de Klerk Wolters, recalling the summer holidays when her family would journey south from their home in the Netherlands to sunny Italy. "My dad would be there too, chatting away with the wine merchants and loving every minute of it." Irene's memories of those Italian adventures still fill her with a sense of wonder. "My parents would take us to mysterious old churches and to the opera in Verona, all of which was absolutely magical to me; honestly, nothing was better than those holidays we spent together in Italy."

Today, Irene has an adventure-loving family of her own. For the past seven years, she and her husband Arjan, together with their sons Beau and Pepijn, have lived and worked in Copenhagen. Moving from Amsterdam to Denmark was a way for the whole family to step outside their cultural comfort zone. Similarly, Irene and Arjan believe that travel is essential for helping their sons to broaden their worldview. So, in the spring of 2019, they decided it was time for the family to return to the many cultural and culinary delights of Italy. The couple designed a loose itinerary that would take them to three distinct regions of Italy where they could sample some of the best that the country had to offer. "Our plan was simple:

The Amalfi Coast is a stretch of coastline on the northern coast of the Salerno Gulf in southern Italy and lies in a Mediterranean climate with warm summers and mild winters.

Aquaglide

QUARANTA

"After the noise of Rome, Puglia felt like another world," says Irene de Klerk Wolters. "With its lovely little villages and rocky beaches, it was the perfect place for us to just go out and play in the sun."

For Irene and her family, there is still magic to be found in Italy. "After all these years, it seems like nothing has changed," she says. "Italy is still as enchanting as ever."

"Our plan was simple: we wanted our boys to see a variety of Italian culture, nature, and daily life. Art and history in Rome, the villages and beaches of Puglia, and the romance of the Amalfi coast."

we wanted our boys to see a variety of Italian culture, nature, and daily life," explains Irene. "Art and history in Rome, the villages and beaches of Puglia, and the romance of the Amalfi coast." The emphasis throughout the holiday, Irene is quick to clarify, was on enjoying Italian food and wine.

The family's first stop on their *tour d'Italia* was Rome. And while Italy's sprawling capital city—with its four million inhabitants and almost 3,000-year history—can be intimidating to travelers with kids, Irene insists it is a must-visit destination. "Even though it's hot and crowded, Rome is unlike any other city in the world; it's basically an open-air museum with this incredible, timeless power to ignite your imagination, no matter how old you are."

Next, the family headed to Puglia, a region that makes up the peninsular heel of Italy's boot. With turquoise seas on all sides and more than 800 kilometers (500 miles) of rugged coastline, Puglia is famed for its curious *trulli* (traditional stone huts with conical roofs) and the local production of bold red wines. "After the noise of Rome, Puglia felt like another world," says Irene. "With its lovely little villages and rocky beaches, it was the perfect place for us to just go out and play in the sun."

For the last week of their holiday, the family traveled to the Amalfi Coast. Designated a UNESCO World Heritage Site, the Amalfi Coast is, for many visitors, the quintessence of postcard-perfect Italy. With its intimate beaches, narrow roads snaking along dramatic cliff edges, and endless tiers of citrus groves rising up from the crystal blue Mediterranean sea, it's no wonder people have loved coming here for generations. On one of their last days in Italy, the family hired a motorboat and spent the day at sea. "Seeing the Amalfi Coast from the water you get a real sense of just how special—how whimsical and unique—this place truly is," Irene says. "I don't think any of us stopped smiling that entire day."

As expected, the highlights from all three legs of the family's journey centered around food. "No matter where we travel, our kids mostly just want to eat," Irene says, "which is great, honestly, because sharing special meals together on holiday forces all of us to slow down and talk about what we're experiencing in that moment." In Rome, they avoided the tourist spots: "We ate with the locals, seated at outdoor tables in quiet piazzas where there was such an incredible atmosphere; it felt like we were in a Fellini movie." In Puglia, one meal in particular stands out: "Our favorite meal was at a seafood restaurant on the beach where we asked the waiter to bring us all of the local specialties; I wouldn't say that the boys liked the taste of everything, but we all loved the experience of surprise and discovery that came with each new, unknown course being served—it was a fantastic evening."

For Irene de Klerk Wolters, there is still magic to be found in Italy. "After all these years, it seems like nothing has changed," she says. "Italy is still as enchanting as ever." Coming back with her own children has given her a new perspective on what makes the country such a special place. "The Italian people are so warm, they really celebrate children and include them in all aspects of life," she says. For Irene, it's this warmth—even between strangers—that allows for the kind of authentic human connections that give traveling its greatest value. And, she adds, "It doesn't hurt that there is the world's best pizza and *gelato* around every corner."

Explore More

THE HEEL OF THE BOOT

Puglia (pronounced poo-li-ya) is a rugged, rural region with a fascinating history, incredible food culture, and lots more to offer intrepid families willing to travel south into "the bootheel" of Italy.

THE BEST COAST

Surprisingly, Puglia is often overlooked by visitors coming to Italy. The region has roughly 800 kilometers (497 miles) of scenic, adventure-ready coastline overlooking the crystal waters of the Adriatic and Ionian Seas.

RICH IN HISTORY

Over the centuries, the Greeks, Romans, Turks, Normans, and French all fought to control Puglia. This means that the region is an archaeological wonderland where medieval castles and Roman sites abound.

"TRULLI" UNIQUE DWELLINGS

The architecture of Puglia's white stone *trulli* dates back to the Middle Ages. Today, many have been converted into guest houses. Visit the town of Alberobello to experience them up close.

COME HUNGRY

Don't miss the *orecchiette* ("little ear" pasta), *burrata*, *tiella* (mussel stew), and *Bombette di Alberobello* (grilled pork stuffed with cheese), sweet *pasticciotto*, and a bottle or two of local Negroamaro wine.

Where the Soul Feels at Home: A Journey toward Conscious Living

EUROPEAN SURF TRIPS

LORETO GALA AND LUTZ SCHWENKE, MAR (11), SOPHIE (7), AND ADA (3)

Inspired to make changes that leave a lasting legacy, one family has combined their love of the sea and sustainable living.

Growing up the child of a Spanish mother and a Chilean father, Loreto Gala often felt as if she were floating between two worlds, "from neither here nor there." After spending the first decade of her life in Spain, Loreto's family moved to Chile, where they stayed for the next 14 years. "My experience living in that small, faraway country has given me a lifelong desire to cross artificial borders and seek out places where my soul feels at home," she says.

Years later, while living in Chile, Loreto met German-born Lutz Schwenke, a passionate surfer, conservationist, and fellow traveler on the journey to discover a more meaningful way of life. The couple fell in love, moved to Hamburg together, and got married. It was during this period that, Loreto says, "I had my first eye-opening exposure to a more conscious life: when I learned to enjoy riding a bicycle, the power of the sun, the awakening of spring, good Italian coffee, the warm glow of candles, the beautiful silence of Christmas, an openness of mind, and a love for things made with my own hands."

In 2010, the couple founded TWOTHIRDS, a sustainable clothing brand that celebrates the surfing lifestyle while actively working to protect and preserve the world's oceans. Since then, the couple has made Barcelona their home and has welcomed three daughters into their family: Mar, Sophie, and Ada, all of

The couple has made Barcelona their home and has welcomed three daughters into their family: Mar, Sophie, and Ada, all of whom share their parents' love for travel, the sea, and the beauty of diversity.

The family organizes their travels with the same conscious, eco-minded approach that they use in their work with TWOTHIRDS. "We stay within Europe and North Africa, and always travel by car to minimize our carbon footprint," says Loreto Gala.

For Loreto and Lutz, the key to conscious living is being thoughtful about the big and small choices they make on a daily basis, from the way they shop for groceries to the ways they run their business, manage their home, or plan a surfing holiday.

"Being a family that originates from different countries has forced us to be more open-minded, more tolerant and adaptable without losing our individual identities. Our kids only know the reality of multiculturalism, so they have a predisposition for traveling, discovery, and learning."

whom share their parents' love for travel, the sea, and the beauty of diversity. On any given day, the family will utilize four languages at home—Spanish, Catalan, German, and English—a reality that poses serious challenges but also brings powerful advantages. "Being a family that originates from different countries has forced us to be more open-minded, more tolerant and adaptable without losing our individual identities," Loreto says. "Often, our children need to put themselves in the shoes of another person and try to understand the way they live." This nuanced sensitivity to diverse perspectives has created a shared love of travel within the Schwenke-Gala household. "Our kids only know the reality of multiculturalism," Loreto says, "so they have a predisposition for traveling, discovery, and learning."

The family regularly gets away together, to make some new memories and, of course, catch some waves. "We don't get great waves around Barcelona," Loreto explains, "so each summer we head toward one of Europe's good surf spots—to Portugal, Cantabria, or the Basque Country." Lutz started teaching Mar and Sophie around the time they each turned six, as soon as they became strong enough swimmers. Before long, it will be Ada's turn to join in the family tradition.

The family organizes their travels with the same conscious, eco-minded approach that they use in their work with TWOTHIRDS. "We stay within Europe and North Africa, and always travel by car to minimize our carbon footprint," Loreto says. "Soon we'll have an electric van, which will reduce our impact even further. We don't need to travel to Indonesia or Hawaii to find good waves or have fun—we definitely want to visit those places someday, but right now we feel that we can take simple steps to reduce our family's impact."

For Loreto and Lutz, the key to conscious living is being thoughtful about the big and small choices they make on a daily basis, from the way they shop for groceries to the ways they run their business, manage their home, or plan a surfing holiday. "Our family goal is to introduce positive changes in people's day-to-day lives," Loreto explains, "through our commitment to the environment, sustainability, the education of our daughters, awareness of existing climate change, and the need to change things for a better world, starting with ourselves." In their experience, it is that combination of conscious living and a sincere love for people and planet that is key to accessing a more meaningful way of life and creating a lasting legacy. "We don't have a rule book or anything, we just try to be loving and compassionate; we believe that the best way to change the world is to show your children how much you love them, as they will treat others the same way and society can change for the better."

Explore More

THOUGHTFUL TRAVEL

The travel choices our families make (and the carbon footprint we create) have an impact on the world of today and tomorrow. Consider how you can make your next family adventure greener.

FLY LESS, FLY SMARTER

If you have to choose air travel, then travel in "economy" whenever you can and bring less luggage. Also, many airlines now have programs where customers can choose to "offset" their carbon footprint.

SUPPORT THE LOCALS

When you travel, use your wallet to support local artisans and small businesses. Avoid chain stores, restaurants, and hotels. You'll not only have a more authentic experience, you'll do some real good as well.

PACK LESS, EXPERIENCE MORE

When prepping for your family's next trip, consider packing less clothes, toys, and gadgets, and, instead, pack more reusable items that will reduce your need to use wasteful, single-use items along the way.

YOUR SUSTAINABLE JOURNEY

Start out by gathering some facts about the environmental impact of travel. Then, set some realistic family goals, and make a plan for how to make your family's future adventures more sustainable.

From the Mountains to the Sea: A Journey Back Home

GARROTXA AND SANT FELIU DE GUÍXOLS (CATALONIA, SPAIN)

LOIS MORENO AND ARNAUD CHEYLUS, ZOÉ (12), HUGO (7), AND SIMON (5)

A Catalan native and her family return to Spain to reconnect with their roots, with nature, and with one another.

"Nature is part of our daily life," says Lois Moreno, whose work as a photographer takes inspiration from her bucolic surroundings. Together with her husband, Arnaud, and their three children, Zoé, Hugo, and Simon, Lois lives in a small country town in France's Loire Valley. Here, Arnaud stays busy renovating the family's historic country house while also working as a trained pastry chef, developing recipes for restaurants around France. The family's idyllic, country lifestyle has woven itself into their relationship to the wider world. "When we travel, we try to understand what makes each region unique. Nature is always part of this connection," Lois explains. "Our planet is our home, and it is important for us that our children learn how to take care of her. What better way to do so than to discover bewildering and majestic landscapes?"

In search of the awe-inspiring power of Mother Earth, in 2018 the family decided to visit Catalonia in Spain. As a child, Lois lived in a tiny fishing village to the south of Barcelona, the region's capital, and spent 20 years residing in the area. Now, she was eager to return with her family. "We hoped to discover another side of Catalonia on this trip," she says. That meant largely skipping Barcelona, even though the city is, as Lois points out, "an infinite source of inspiration." Instead, the family looked toward lesser-traveled regions, places even Lois had never been before. With

The family fell so in love with the landscapes of Garrotxa that one day they decided to experience them in a new way: from the air. "In the very early morning, we took to the skies in a hot-air balloon," Lois says. "It was an exceptional adventure."

Just 120 kilometers (75 miles) north of Barcelona, the natural landforms of Garrotxa have been molded by the constant subterranean activity that gave rise to its 40 volcanoes.

The holiday not only broadened the children's appreciation of nature, but also encouraged their understanding of family history. "Catalonia is part of who we are as a family. Exploring this region deepened our feelings of pride and attachment," says Lois Moreno.

"Our planet is our home, and it is important for us that our children learn how to take care of her. What better way to do so than to discover bewildering and majestic landscapes?"

nature as their focus, they decided to split the journey into two chapters: first, the family would explore the volcanic landscapes of inland Garrotxa, and then travel to the stunning seascapes of coastal Sant Feliu de Guíxols.

Just 120 kilometers (75 miles) north of Barcelona, the natural landforms of Garrotxa have been molded by the constant subterranean activity that gave rise to its 40 volcanoes, none of which, reassuringly, have erupted in the past 11,000 years. Besides that, the region is famed for its medieval towns of stone and the production of goat cheese. "I was surprised by the beauty of Garrotxa," Lois admits. "Unique landscapes, gorgeous walks, charming small towns, endless paths, wheat fields, and welcoming people—happiness everywhere!" The family stayed in the west of the region, in the town of La Vall d'en Bas, and frequently set out to explore the area's abundant nature walks. "We really enjoyed discovering them all together and creating wonderful memories," Lois says.

The family fell so in love with the volcanic landscapes of Garrotxa that one day they decided to experience them in a new way: from the air. "In the early morning, very early, we took to the skies in a hot-air balloon," Lois says. An activity that offers a bird's-eye view of craters and landslides, rusty earth and ancient lava flows. Hot-air ballooning is becoming increasingly popular in Garrotxa. "There is the silence and extraordinary beauty of the landscape, a unique landscape with a thousand contrasts," Lois says. "It was an exceptional adventure that will remain etched in our memories."

After the climactic heights of their visit to Garrotxa, the family made a short trip south to the coastal town of Sant Feliu de Guíxols, where they encountered a dramatic change in scenery: sandy beaches, rocky coves, and forests of pine and oak trees. Situated beside the crystal clear waters of the Mediterranean, the quaint town offers a variety of sea-based activities like snorkeling, kayaking, and boating. But Lois and her family decided to keep things grounded on this second leg of the journey. "The beaches and coves are ideal for lounging in the sun, and the town has a historic center filled with pedestrian alleys, ideal for strollers," she says. They took time just to wander around, take in the sea views, and stop every now and again for a cold beer and an ice cream.

"Traveling with children is an incredible experience that invites you to discover and share," says Lois. "Learning with others really nourishes the spirit and the soul." As they traveled between the rugged volcanic terrain of Garrotxa and the serene coast of Sant Feliu de Guíxols, the family formed new bonds with the natural world. "The sea and the mountains coexist harmoniously," Lois says. "We feel connected to nature, no matter where we are." This particular holiday, she says, not only broadened her children's appreciation of nature, but also encouraged their understanding of family history. "Catalonia is part of who we are as a family," she says. "Exploring unknown parts of this rich and contrasted region deepened our feelings of pride and attachment." Despite having spent 20 years of her life in Catalonia, returning with her family was a good reminder that there is always more to discover about where you come from—more adventures to be had and new memories to create with the people you love.

Explore More

WELCOME TO CATALONIA
This unique "nation within Spain" consists of four provinces: Girona, Lleida, Tarragona, and Barcelona. Many people here speak Catalan (as well as Spanish) and believe strongly in Catalonian independence.

MAKE BARCELONA YOUR BASE
Barcelona is home to mountains, beaches, castles, ancient streets, and some of the most stunning architecture in the world. The capital of Catalonia makes a perfect base for exploring the region.

PACK CAREFULLY
With the Pyrenees at the region's northern border and the Mediterranean Sea to the east, the climate of Catalonia features hot summers and cooler, wetter, and snowier winters than the rest of Spain.

AVENTURAS NATURALES
From swimming with tuna in l'Ametlla de Mar, to crushing grapes in Vilafranca, to exploring the l'Espluga caves, to cycling the region's kid-friendly greenways, there is far more to the region than beaches.

POSTCARD-WORTHY PLACES
These picturesque towns are well worth a visit: coastal Calella de Palafrugell, medieval Besalu, enchanting Peratallada, Tossa de Mar, traffic-free Rupit, and Cadaques, known as "the pearl of Costa Brava."

The Journey Is the Thing: Epic Days under Sail in the Ionian Sea

IONIAN ISLANDS, GREECE

ANTONIA AND TOMMY CHABROWSKI, CHLOE (8) AND LUCAS (5)

For the last leg of a European vacation, an American family sets sail for a week of adventure in the Greek islands.

Tommy and Antonia Chabrowski both grew up traveling the world, first with their own parents, then on their own, and, later, with each other. Antonia, who was born in Bulgaria, spent several childhood summers traveling back to Europe to visit family. In the early 2000s, Tommy spent five years on an "endless summer"-style surfing odyssey. "When we met, we had this deep, shared love of travel," Antonia says. "Then we had kids, and, honestly, not much has changed."

"We are a physical, adventurous family, and we love everything from swimming to biking to skiing and even roller coasters." Yet, one adventure that had long eluded the Chabrowskis, was a sailing journey through the Greek islands. In 2019, when their youngest child turned five, they felt that their kids were finally old enough for an adventure at sea. Now, they just needed to find a ship, a crew, and a captain.

Luckily, the family already knew an expert on sailing in the Greek isles—their Brooklyn neighbor, Ross Beane, the co-founder and operations coordinator for the luxury charter company Sailing Collective, which operates holidays throughout the Caribbean, Europe, and Asia. "We had seen Ross's photos and heard about the trips he put together, so we were really excited to try one out," says Antonia. So, in August 2019, they embarked on a big European

HONDA
Oceanis 50

"When Tommy and I met, we had this deep, shared love of travel. Then we had kids, and, honestly, not much has changed. We are a physical, adventurous family, and we love everything from swimming to biking to skiing and even roller coasters," says Antonia Chabrowski.

"We would start each day with a family plunge," Antonia Chabrowski recalls, "and then anytime the boat would stop, Tommy and I would jump in with the kids a few times. But, I swear, they must have jumped in and climbed out 100 times a day."

For more than 3,000 years, voyagers have been coming to Greece's western islands: settlers and traders, soldiers and sailors, artists and adventurers. These islands are places haunted by millennia of mythology. The seas that surround them are some of the most enchanting in the world.

"There is just something magical about spending time at sea," reflects Antonia Chabrowski. "Being together on that boat, you can really, fully let go and be right in the moment; somehow it's relaxing and exciting all at once."

Before heading to bed each night, the family would take a few minutes to lay on deck and look up at the sky together. "Lying there, all of us together, looking up at the stars each night was so beautiful. It was just so surreal."

adventure that took the family from New York to Berlin, then to Mallorca, Spain, and, finally, to Corfu, Greece, where a Sailing Collective crew was waiting to welcome the family on board for a week of cruising in the Ionian Sea. They were joined by two other families for the trip: "There were eleven of us in total, five kids and six adults," Antonia explains. "All of us had traveled together before, so we knew that the kids would have just as much fun together as the parents; it was a really solid group to be in close quarters with." For the next seven days and nights, the families made themselves at home aboard *The Melina,* a 48-foot catamaran that would carry them from Corfu to Paxos, and then to Parga and Sivota Mourtos on the Greek mainland, before returning to Corfu. Under the supervision of the vessel's expert crew, Antonia, Tommy, and the kids spent the week lounging on deck, fishing off the bow, learning basic seamanship, and swimming in the crystalline waters of the Ionian Sea.

A favorite memory from the family's voyage was their daily ritual of jumping into the sea together. Each day—several times a day, in fact—mom, dad, sister, and brother would pluck up their courage and then, hands held, leap from the deck of the boat into the clear, warm water below. Each time, Antonia remembers, all four Chabrowskis came up out of the water smiling. "We would start each day with a family plunge," Antonia recalls, "and then anytime the boat would stop, Tommy and I would jump in with the kids a few times. But, I swear, they must have jumped in and climbed out 100 times a day."

Throughout the voyage, the ship's chef, Vivian, kept passengers and crew well-fed with a carefully curated menu that featured fresh-caught fish, produce sourced from the ship's various ports of call, and special kid-friendly meals. "Before we arrived on Corfu, we had filled out a food questionnaire that Vivian had obviously studied really closely," Antonia explains. "She was amazing in the kitchen and the food was absolutely insane." On board, dinner would often begin around 9:00 p.m., several hours later than normal for the Chabrowski kids. But, as Antonia says, that was all part of the holiday experience. "We let go a little bit and relaxed," she says, "some nights the kids went to bed at midnight and, you know what, that was totally fine." Before heading to bed each night, the family would take a few minutes to lay on deck and look up at the sky together. "Lying there, all of us together, looking up at the stars each night was so beautiful," Antonia recalls. "It was just so surreal."

Before their trip to Greece, "Tommy had sailed in his past, and I had been on a few day trips before," Antonia says, "but nothing like this. Everything about our time in the islands was incredible: the views, the company, the food. Our kids were always entertained and loved being on the boat. The whole experience was so freeing, and it was just such a surreal experience to travel this way."

At week's end, the Chabrowskis said goodbye to their travel mates and the crew of *The Melina.* After a short stopover in Athens, they returned home to New York with some jet lag, a bit of sunburn, and their memories still aglow from their first family sailing adventure. "There is just something magical about spending time at sea," Antonia reflects. "Being together on that boat, you can really, fully let go and be right in the moment; somehow it's relaxing and exciting all at once." In other words, she says, sailing with her family in the Greek islands was "absolutely epic."

Explore More

A LAND OF MYTH

Also known as the Heptanese, the Ionian Islands were named for Io, the mythological princess and mortal lover of Zeus. Although a longtime possession of the Venetian empire, the islands became part of Greece in 1864.

THE ENCHANTED ISLES

From north to south, Corfu, Paxos, Lefkas, Ithaca, Cefalonia, Zante, and Cythera each have something to offer travelers of all ages; from isolated beaches to mountain vistas and seaside tavernas.

EPIC CUISINE

Influenced by centuries of Venetian rule, Ionian cuisine is a dream of rustic breads, fragrant sauces, fish stew, lush cheeses, kumquat liqueurs, garlic sauces, and wines made from dozens of grape varieties.

TAKE THE HELM

For millennia, boating has been central to life in the Ionian Islands. Most of the islands' towns offer rentals and guidance on how to safely explore the scenic coastlines, coves, and hidden beaches by boat.

REQUIRED READING

The *Odyssey* still has the power to enchant intrepid readers of all ages. For the grown-ups, *My Family and Other Animals* by the English naturalist Gerald Durrell is a humorous memoir set in 1930s Corfu.

Deep in the Heart of Texas: A Search for the Perfect Swimming Hole

BARTON SPRINGS, TEXAS, USA

SARA AND BILLY JACK BRAWNER, ELLSWORTH (9), FLORA (8), BILLY JACK (7), PACE (7), AND JONES (3)

A Texas family heads outdoors to explore the wonders of nature, create new memories, and grow closer together.

Once upon a time—back when he was a university student—Billy Jack Brawner went backpacking in Morocco and, while exploring the baked deserts, rugged mountains, and dusty medinas of North Africa, he developed a personal mantra: "If I see water, I'm going to jump into it."

Many years (and five kids) later, Billy Jack's love for wild swimming has become a passion shared by his entire family—a passion that has inspired the Brawner clan to explore their home state of Texas in an ongoing quest to find the perfect summer swimming hole.

Although Billy Jack grew up in a place where wild swimming wasn't really an option, Sara Brawner is from just outside of Austin, where a number of pristine, natural oases welcome adventurous swimmers throughout the year. "When we were dating, we would spend as much time as possible swimming in the nearby rivers and cliff-jumping into the springs," says Billy Jack. "It's genuinely our favorite thing to do together." The couple's long-standing love of swimming in nature has been passed on to their five children: Ellsworth, Flora, Billy Jack, Pace, and Jones. Both parents say there is something profoundly

Over the years, the Brawners have sought out a number of the Lone Star State's best swimming holes, from the Texas Hill Country to the Blanco River, north of San Antonio. But the current family favorite is Barton Springs in the heart of Austin.

“Getting to see each other in new environments, with new challenges, helps all of us learn more about one another,” says Billy Jack Brawner. “Making new memories and coming up with ‘you had to be there’ inside jokes truly unifies us.”

"You can never tell when the magic is gonna strike. An adventure that's well planned seems to have about the same success rate as a completely spontaneous one. In fact, we've learned that some of the best adventures are the imperfect ones."

beautiful about watching their children fall in love with the same natural wonders that they themselves were fascinated with as kids. "Touching the slimy algae, feeling minnows swim between your toes, looking for baby turtles sunning on the shore, and floating on your back while watching the light filter through the cypress trees overhead—it's pure magic," says Billy Jack.

Over the past few years, the Brawners have sought out a number of the Lone Star State's best swimming holes, especially those found in the Texas Hill Country, including Blue Hole, Jacob's Well, and Cypress Creek—all near Wimberley, Texas—and the Blanco River, north of San Antonio. But the current family favorite is Barton Springs—a series of four natural springs located inside Austin's Zilker Park. "We love Barton Springs and all the beautiful little spots tucked away along Austin's greenbelt—crystal clear, refreshing waters with towering cypress trees on either bank," says Billy Jack. "It's the best of the best, so we try to get the family there as much as possible."

What does it take for a family of seven to enjoy a full day of fun, safe, outdoor adventure in Texas? Sara Brawner explains the key is to keep things simple. "Water bottles and protein bars for everybody, sunscreen, and sturdy water shoes are basically all we need," she says, "and then we always have to remind the kids to be on the lookout for poison ivy, poison oak, and snakes." In the course of their quest for the perfect swimming hole, the Brawner family has had a few misadventures as well, including some close calls with snakes and one very notable navigational mishap. "One day, we went into the forest for a hike and got lost for six hours without food or water, with four kids under eight and a 13-month-old baby," Sara remembers. Despite the fear, exhaustion, and frustration of wandering the woods for hours, the family came together and made the most of this potentially traumatic episode. "Honestly, that was maybe one of the most unifying days for our family," says Billy Jack, "and, toward the end of the day, we even found an incredible waterfall and a perfect little swimming hole."

For the Brawner family, a commitment to long nature hikes and seeking out the perfect swimming holes is part of a larger investment in growing and strengthening their relationships with one another. "Getting to see each other in new environments, with new challenges, helps all of us learn more about one another," says Billy Jack. "Making new memories and coming up with 'you had to be there' inside jokes truly unifies us." Sara believes these adventures are not only formative for their kids, but also for her and Billy Jack as parents. "When we have these shared experiences, they become family landmarks that we can—and often do—look back upon fondly," she says. "And then a crazy, six-hour hike that requires our son to trust us even though he's bleeding and crying and hungry, ultimately helps him to trust us a little more with a very normal problem on a normal Tuesday back home in Waco."

Explore More

AUSTIN: A WILD WEST OASIS

A vibrant city that combines the energy of a university town with Texas politics, a thriving music scene, and some of the state's best opportunities for outdoor fun, the unofficial local motto is "Keep Austin Weird."

BARTON CREEK GREENBELT

From natural spring pools (a constant 21°C [70°F] all year) to hiking trails, mountain biking, rock climbing, and waterfall jumping, this beloved scenic area offers so much for outdoor enthusiasts.

BEER, BBQ, AND TACOS

Craft beer, Texas-style barbecue, and Tex-Mex are Austin's best known specialties. Start with Franklin for BBQ, Veracruz All Natural for tacos. As for the beers—you'll just have to try them all.

DEEP IN THE HEART OF TEXAS

Hidden for millennia, the amazing Inner Space Cavern, located north of Austin, was first discovered by the Texas Highway Department in 1963. This well-preserved cave has lots to inspire kids of all ages.

HEAD FOR COVER

When it gets too hot, head for air-conditioned cover in one of Austin's many inspiring museums, such as the Thinkery (science space for kids) or Contemporary Austin: Laguna Gloria (a kid-friendly art museum).

“From our experience, the more curious, flexible, and resilient we can be as parents, the more our kids mirror us and rise to the challenge of whatever happens,” says Billy Jack.

TRAVEL TIPS: THREE TO SIX

Three- to six-year-olds are acutely interested in their surrounding environment. They pore over insects, plants, rocks, and food—basically anything they can get their hands on—stretching out even the most routine trip. This becomes even more of a factor when traveling in unfamiliar places and can put pressure on your schedule, so plan in extra time for dillydallying. This way a child of this age range can discover all they want to, and a parent can exercise that invaluable virtue of patience, without worrying about missing the next part of the journey.

Choosing a Destination

Traveling with children in these formative years will have a lasting impact on how they come to view future journeys. If you want to ensure eagerly anticipated and pleasant trips to come, try to choose a destination that you know your child will really enjoy.

Natural environments—beaches, lakes or rivers, and forest settings—provide endless opportunities for fun and exploration. But a city destination is not out of the question.

Many public institutions, such as natural history and science museums, have learning facilities designed for children of preschool and early school ages—places where, with your overseeing eye, they can further develop their learning skills.

How to Get There

Routine is everything with children in this age group, and any form of travel will likely interrupt the flow of that calming and familiar day-to-day reality. One way to ease the disruption is to simply tell your child the plan in a way they can understand—this opens the door to the "remember what we spoke about" act.

The other more practical option for short trips is to try to orient travel time around naptime. At best, you'll get through an entire journey without your child waking, and at worst, they will at least have slept for part of it.

But beware: motion sickness becomes a factor to consider for children over two years old, so make sure you bring some plastic bags.

Checklist (For City Trips)

- Travel documents (insurance, boarding passes, passports, etc.)
- Written itinerary
- Car seat
- Clothes (one set for each day, plus a few extras)
- Hats (with neck protection)
- Pyjamas
- Sippy cups
- Children's toothbrushes
- Pull-ups (for long journeys)
- Travel potty
- Crayons and coloring and children's books
- Toys and games
- Plastic bags (for wet items of clothing and motion sickness emergencies)
- Blankets
- Snacks
- Lollipops (to relieve air pressure on flights)
- Travel first aid kit
- Digital thermometer
- Medications (prescriptions and children's acetaminophen or ibuprofen)
- Nasal saline drops
- Tissues
- Electronic devices (tablet, smartphone, portable DVD player)
- Universal sink stopper (for accommodations without their own)

Where to Sleep

When visiting urban areas, booking hotels, bed-and-breakfasts, or private homes will be a necessary part of the process. As children are often able to sleep in their own beds by this point, you probably won't have to worry about cots. But if you want to avoid an overcrowded bed, book larger hotel rooms with foldout sofa beds, which are perfect for children in this age range. If you book a private home, make sure there are enough beds for everybody. And remember to inspect the host's photos carefully: try to avoid residences that have a lot of breakable decorative items around the place, or lock objects like these away in a cupboard once you arrive.

Where to Eat

As with even younger children, seeking out the earliest possible reservation time at a restaurant will mean an all-round more enjoyable dining experience. Still, you might only want to do this once a day. So what about lunch? Go to a local grocer and buy a store of supplies that will last a few days. Stock up on healthy options for light meals—think simple sandwiches, fruit snacks, and covetable treats. This style of lunching will eliminate one extra burden in an already busy schedule and also allow you to be mobile during the day. To lessen resistance to new foods, introduce items you expect to find at your destination into your child's diet before you leave.

How to Move Around

Traveling locally becomes a little easier with children in this age range. You will probably have left the stroller behind, so public buses, trains, and trams are that much more accessible. But you do have to keep in mind that undertaking lengthy day trips can be tiring for both you and your child: once they stop wanting to walk, you might have to carry them. You can avoid this by bringing along a folding scooter or balance bike.

If you have the luggage space, these handy gadgets can be taken apart and packed into suitcases. Some companies also offer ride-on travel suitcases, which can make transit zones that much more fun for children.

Unexpected Twists

Whether you're traveling by sea, rail, or road, motion sickness can become a problem for children in this age group. If you know your child is sensitive to motion while traveling, try to sit in seats that feel more stable, such as the front section or near the wings of a plane. In the case of train travel, sit near a window.

Dramamine for kids helps to keep food down, but that's not always possible, so ensure that your child does not eat anything that could create stomach problems before you travel. Take breaks from screens, walk around, and let air circulate. And even if your child is not known to have motion sickness, bring watertight plastic bags just in case.

Hack

Children often become restless in transit, particularly if the journey is a long one, but a simple game can be a saving grace. Choose one that doesn't contain a jumble of individual parts—they're likely to get lost. A popular choice is the perennially fascinating magnetic drawing board, which commonly goes by the brand name Magna Doodle.

Not only can your child simply doodle away on these, but they are also the perfect platform for classic, endlessly repeating games such as tic-tac-toe or hangman. The more up-to-date versions of these drawing toys are called "boogie boards." They feature LCD screens that can be erased with the simple push of a button, and some offer the option of saving the board's contents.

Pure Magic: Moments of Wonder in the Hawaiian Islands

HAWAIIAN ISLANDS, USA

MARIELLE AND TK MCKAMY, AND MAVERICK (1)

After becoming parents, a pair of carefree travelers returns to paradise in search of a new kind of travel magic.

Before becoming parents, TK and Marielle McKamy never missed a chance for spontaneous adventure. "On a whim, we'd hit the road and head off to Big Sur or Joshua Tree or Zion National Park in Utah," TK recalls, "any place where we could reconnect with each other and with nature." These trips were more than just exciting, TK explains, "they fed our souls and refreshed our minds." But no adventures have been more refreshing or inspiring than the couple's trips to Hawaii.

"The first time we ever went to Hawaii together, it was a completely spontaneous getaway," recalls TK, an LA-based film and music video director. "We had only been dating a few weeks at that point, but we hopped on a plane and headed to the North Shore of Oahu." During that first trip, TK and Marielle felt entirely carefree. Each morning, the couple would wake up early and visit the local food trucks. Then, they'd swim away the days, floating in the surf with sea turtles and cliff jumping. In the evenings, they cruised around the island, visiting the best restaurants, eating poke bowls, and drinking tropical cocktails. "The whole island life is like some kind of irresistible call of the wild," says TK. "It's just pure magic."

Since that first trip, the couple has made several return visits to Hawaii. Over the years, the islands have become intimately

"Now we find that we need to slow down a lot more and take time to really enjoy the simple things: introducing Mavi to the beach and the rocks, sharing an açái bowl, or watching the sunset together—these moments of wonder are the reasons that we travel as a family," says Marielle McKamy.

Along with introducing their daughter to the wonders of the wide world, the McKamys are also committed to teaching her the value of spontaneous, everyday adventure—the kinds of whimsical, soul-feeding experiences at the very heart of their family story.

"We believe there is so much to learn from stepping out of the comforts of our native culture and context; the experience is always a challenge—it's exciting but it's also life-giving."

entwined with the arc of their family story; this was the place the pair was married in 2016, and where they celebrated their first wedding anniversary. "It's absolutely our favorite place in the whole world," says TK, "the perfect combination of slow, country living and lush, otherworldly landscapes." The couple feels right at home on "island time," and readily embrace the laid-back, "no shoes, no shirt, no problem," mentality that Hawaii is famous for. "It's such a special place," TK says. "As long as you treat the land and the people with the utmost respect, you will always enjoy your time in Hawaii."

These days, when the McKamys make trips back to Hawaii, the journey is still a magical one, albeit somewhat less spontaneous with their young daughter, Maverick, in tow. "The experience is just as sweet as always," says Marielle, "but now we find that we need to slow down a lot more and take time to really enjoy the simple things: introducing Mavi to the beach and the rocks, sharing an acai bowl with her or watching the sunset together—these moments of wonder are the reasons that we travel as a family." Since Maverick was born, the McKamys have learned to simplify and let go of a lot of the things they once thought their daughter would "need" when traveling. "The more we travel with Mavi, the more we learn to travel with less stuff," says TK. "She doesn't need all that extra gear for sleeping, eating, and playing; when we travel, we simplify, adapt, and just make it work. Besides, as long as our kid has a piece of smoked swordfish jerky in her hand, she's the happiest girl on the island."

TK and Marielle hope that, by regularly exposing their daughter to new places, different cultures, and shared moments of wonder, she will grow up with an inquisitive and deeply empathetic character. "We believe there is so much to learn from stepping out of the comforts of our native culture and context; the experience is always a challenge—it's exciting but it's also life-giving," says TK. When their daughter was born, Marielle explains, "We named our little girl Maverick because we hope she will grow up to resist fear and conformity and that she will be outgoing and adventurous throughout her life." As she gets older, they hope to travel with Mavi to Japan, Bali, Africa, Europe, and elsewhere. Of course, they also hope to continue returning to Hawaii, so that as she grows up, the magical islands that her parents have loved so well will also have a uniquely sacred place in Mavi's own life's story.

Along with introducing their daughter to the wonders of the wide world, the McKamys are also committed to teaching her the value of spontaneous, everyday adventure—the kinds of whimsical, soul-feeding experiences at the very heart of their family story. "There's a favorite refrain you'll often hear around our house," TK says, "safe has plans, crazy has stories."

Explore More

ALOHA, OAHU!

Oahu is the third largest of the Hawaiian Islands. In the winter, the island hosts championship big wave surfing. From May to September each year, calmer seas entice five million tourists to visit paradise.

THE PERFECT DAY

Gear up and grab coffee in the historic surf town of Haleiwa before hiking the kid-friendly Ka'ena Point Trail or heading off to swim in Waimea Bay. Afterwards, treat yourselves to some Hawaiian "shave ice."

YOU GOTTA TASTE THIS

The açaí bowl has been a staple surfer food in Hawaii for decades. Made from pureed Brazilian açaí berries, these fresh, earthy bowls are colorful, flavorful, and loaded with antioxidants.

AN ADVENTURE PARADISE

Along with surfing, swimming, and snorkeling in the waters around Oahu, there are countless outdoor activities to do with kids in Hawaii, including hiking, horseback riding, and dolphin and whale watching.

REQUIRED READING

Letters from Hawaii by Mark Twain, *Ancient History of the Hawaiian People* by Abraham Fornander, *Captive Paradise* by James L. Haley, and *Hawaiian Legends for Little Ones* by Gabrielle Ahuli'i.

From the Eternal Desert to the Atlas Mountains: A Journey in Morocco

MARRAKECH, THE AGAFAY DESERT, AND THE ATLAS MOUNTAINS (MOROCCO)

KINE ASK STENERSEN AND KRISTOFFER ENG, VILMER (5) AND ARTUR (1)

A Norwegian family escapes the Nordic winter and travels to Morocco in search of sun, adventure, and inspiration.

Discovering new experiences in unfamiliar cultures is one of the keys to awakening creative inspiration. This is especially true for Kine Ask Stenersen and Kristoffer Eng, the husband and wife duo behind the Norwegian design studio Ask og Eng. "Traveling was a big part of our lives before kids," says Kine, whose designs focus on weaving distinctive Nordic craftsmanship into sustainable, high-quality kitchens and furniture. Kristoffer is an architect by trade who studied in Århus, Denmark and Kine is an environmental geographer who studied in Bergen and Buenos Aires. Today the couple shares a design studio in Oslo and a workshop in Drammen where they construct sleek, minimalist kitchens and furniture from bamboo. Crafting spaces together sparked a deep love for the creative process that set the course for the couple's design journey. In 2018, they decided to embark on their first design adventure as a family, a two-week-long journey through Morocco with their sons Vilmer and Artur.

"For this trip, we wanted to get away from winter in Norway, have some quality time as a family, and find inspiration for new projects," says Kine. But stepping out of their highly structured Scandinavian life to voyage into North Africa with their children was an adventure met with some trepidation. "The flight attendant on the way over remarked, 'You're really adventurous, I would never

Kine and Kristoffer's advice for families who want to follow their lead was to focus on what interests you the most. "What we thought may be challenging for the kids ended up being what they liked the most and is what they still talk about," says Kine.

"What we thought may be challenging for the kids ended up being what they liked the most and is what they still talk about. It was a good way for the kids to learn to be tolerant and more open as they see and experience more of the world."

“When we arrived, we experienced the chaos that occurs in Marrakech right away, the smell of spices and animals really hit us, there were people everywhere, and I could see that the kids were overwhelmed. I couldn’t help but think, what have we done?” says Kine Ask Stenersen.

"Seeing the mysterious Atlas Mountains, living in a tent for a few days, and staying up late as we sat around the bonfire and looked up at the stars were such huge experiences for all of us. It truly was unforgettable."

bring my kids to Marrakech,' and that really made us feel nervous," Kine says. For some, the hustle and bustle of Morocco can be polarizing if you aren't prepared. "When we arrived, we experienced the chaos that occurs in Marrakech right away: the smell of spices and animals really hit us, there were people everywhere, and I could see that the kids were overwhelmed. Our driver pulled up and started yelling, 'C'mon, c'mon!' It takes a bit more to throw me off, but being there with two young kids, I couldn't help but think, 'What have we done?'" But once the family arrived at their hotel and got settled in, they soon saw why Morocco has become a favorite destination for those seeking the resilient charm of a bygone era.

"When we got to Riad 42, it was paradise—there were birds singing and the hosts welcomed us with open arms and, of course, tea," Kine says. The picturesque resort channels the essence of traditional Moroccan homes with courtyards that seamlessly intertwine Old World design with modern amenities. The founders designed the space with meticulous care to provide guests a window into the deeply social nature of local customs, such as conversing over meals and tea. "Because it was a small riad, only five or six rooms, we had breakfast and dinner with many wonderful new people," says Kine. "Just last month we had a visitor here in Norway who we met in Riad 42." Kine explains that one key to traveling with their young sons was to try and stay even-keeled. "Our main goal was to relax, not stress too much, and take things really slow. We also spent quite a lot of time inside the riad unwinding." Additionally, the family's careful planning helped strike the right balance of relaxing, exploring, and finding design inspiration in the exotic atmosphere. "We did quite a lot of research beforehand and hired a local guide to help us find the markets and shops that sold the ceramics and wooden products we hoped for." But some of the best experiences are those you can't plan for, especially when it comes to guessing what your children will love. After taking in the carnival of spices, fresh fruits, and antiques in Marrakech's old medina, the family embarked for Scarabeo Camp, a luxurious campsite in the Agafay desert set against the Atlas Mountains. "This is the place that our five-year-old still talks about," says Kine. "It made such an impression on him seeing that desert, staying out till late, and sleeping in tents." A highlight for the whole family was a candlelit dinner beneath a starlit sky as a campfire warmed the cool of the desert night. Next they ventured to the Atlas Mountains, a refreshing change from their trip so far. "Going from the desert to the mountains was an incredible contrast," Kine says. "Everything was suddenly so lush and green; it was a breathtaking place."

Looking back, Kine and Kristoffer's advice for families who want to follow their lead was to focus on what interests you the most. "What we thought may be challenging for the kids ended up being what they liked the most and is what they still talk about," says Kine. As parents, the trip had a profound impact on Kine and Kristoffer: "This experience gave us so many insights. It was a good way for the kids to learn to be tolerant and more open as they see and experience more of the world." As designers, the shared meals with new friends in lush gardens, quick bites eaten in the clamor of the medina, and dinners *en plein air* under desert starlight are unforgettable moments that will undoubtedly help to shape the future of Ask og Eng—both as a design team and as a family of adventurous travelers.

Explore More

"RED CITY," EST. 1062 CE
The city's ancient medina is walled in by 6-meter- (20-foot-) tall ramparts made of red clay bricks, giving the city its nickname "red city." Built in the 12th century, the walls feature 20 gates and 200 towers.

WHEN TO VISIT
The heat during the high summer—from June to August—can be intense, so fall and spring are better times to visit. Also, make sure to double-check the dates of Ramadan (which change each year).

STAY AT A MOROCCAN RIAD
A riad is a traditional home with an interior courtyard or garden based on historic Mediterranean or Middle Eastern architecture. Today, many riads in Marrakech are operated as family-friendly guest houses.

TAKE MOM TO A HAMMAM
There are public and private hammams (Middle Eastern steam baths) found throughout Marrakech, all of which feature a relaxing atmosphere, vigorous massage, natural oils, and plenty of invigorating steam.

ADVENTURE BASE
Sandboarding on the dunes, motorcycle tours, camel rides, ATV desert tours, glamping under the stars beside the Atlas Mountains, Marrakech is an incredible base for North African adventure.

A Year Interrupted

by Oliver Jeffers

"We could move depending on our mood, but mostly because we were realizing the most beautiful moments happened not from solid planning, or from ticking the box of seeing all the things that are supposed to be seen."

We were entering our seventh month in what was supposed to be a year of travel with our two young children when a global pandemic hit. We retreated to Belfast—not where we normally live—to enter lockdown closer to family, and have isolated ourselves in an apartment for three months now. Reflecting back on our voyage, I don't think travel will ever be the same again.

For one thing, will we ever again be comfortable to the point of blasé sitting in such close proximity to so many strangers in a contained environment for the duration of, say, a trans-Atlantic flight? Or happily use public bathrooms in a restaurant or hotel?

There were early signs of just how quickly the planet responded to the lack of emissions from car commuting and air traveling: mountains visible in the distant horizon that had before been obscured by smog, the water in the Venice canals becoming clear enough to see the bottom. It begs the questions of how we will travel in the future, and how we can create an industry of responsible tourism, so our kids can travel when they grow up to the sorts of places we do (or did) without wreaking the havoc (locally and globally) that we have.

Looking at the empty skies, the empty roads, and imagining all those empty hotels, it seems a world ago that we set off from Brooklyn—our home for the last decade—and sailed across the Atlantic to begin our voyage, not knowing where exactly we were going. The entirety of our planning for the period building up to departure was all about clearing the space to leave, rather than figuring out what we would do once gone. There were certainly moments when it felt like we were dragging our children kicking and screaming across the cities of the globe (frankly that is often exactly what we were doing—a one-year-old and a four-year-old don't have much patience for anything other than exactly what they want "right now"). As frustrating as this was at times, causing us to ask ourselves periodically why we were doing it at all, we learned to be grateful for our initial lack of a solid plan—partly because we could move depending on our mood, but mostly because we were realizing the most beautiful moments happened not from solid planning, or from ticking the box of seeing all the things that are supposed to be seen. They came instead from the small, accidental moments, in not very obvious places, where things fell into place and contentment settled upon us. Like the time we arrived in southern Italy, drove for three hours to a rental house, and realized we had not thought about dinner. We drove around a small industrial town all closed up on a Monday night, looking for anywhere that would feed us. The only place open was a small pizza cafe. We sat ourselves down for what turned out to be the best (and cheapest) pizza we had ever eaten, in what also turned out to be the social center for retired men in the area, coming to life around us as we ate. Or, the time my son and I cleared out of the motel room we were staying in along the Oregon coast so my daughter could take a nap. We found our way along the rocky shore to a perfect sandy alcove that gave us shelter from the late winter wind. We huddled and played there, watching the waves crash nearby, and an hour later, somehow my wife and our daughter wandered the same way. I went back to grab a bottle of wine and makeshift picnic and we stayed in our little hidden spot to watch the sun go down. We recognized enough to just sit and savor these moments. We were noticing that it didn't take very much to make us happy.

"One thing this pandemic has taught us is that maybe we travel too easily, too thoughtlessly, over vast distances to chase a feeling, without asking ourselves why, or really considering the consequences global movement like this has on local culture or ecosystems."

One thing this pandemic has taught us is that maybe we travel too easily, too thoughtlessly, over vast distances to chase a feeling, without asking ourselves why, or really considering the consequences global movement like this has on local culture or ecosystems—and who or what we leave behind when we do. The joy of a simple home-cooked meal with family doesn't require traveling halfway around the world.

Perhaps it wasn't the world we had taken a year off to see. We'd taken it to see ourselves.

"It begs the questions of how we will travel in the future, and how we can create an industry of responsible tourism, so our kids can travel when they grow up to the sorts of places we do (or did) without wreaking the havoc (locally and globally) that we have."

OLIVER JEFFERS is a Brooklyn based, Northern Irish artist and author working in painting, bookmaking, illustration, collage, performance, and sculpture. His critically acclaimed picture books have been translated into over 45 languages, while his artwork is exhibited internationally.

There and Back Again: Discovering Community 9,000 Miles from Home

While waiting for the adoption of their daughter to be finalized, an American couple establishes a home away from home on the shores of Uganda's Lake Victoria and learns the true meaning of family, friendship, and community.

MARY AND JP MCLEOD, AND THEIR TWO DAUGHTERS (AGES 3 AND 8)

Mary McLeod's camera clicked as she captured the moment everything changed. She was in Jinja, Uganda, two hours east of the capital city of Kampala and 14,484 kilometers (9,000 miles) from her home in California. She had been invited to photograph a friend's family as they met the children they would soon adopt. There, near the source of the River Nile, Mary fell in love. "It is a slow-paced town," she says, "where everyone walks and rides on the back of *boda bodas* for transport. I knew I wanted to come back when a camera wasn't in my hands all the time." Eight months later, she did exactly that.

Mary grew up in Florida but spent her young adult life in California, where she went to college to study psychology before pivoting into photography. In December of 2012, she took a break from her growing business, gave away most of her belongings, and returned to Jinja to volunteer with various local organizations for six months. While she was there, a visit by a friend from home turned into a first date with her future husband, JP—the two were engaged soon after Mary returned to the United States, and married within a year. Mary's love for Uganda soon became the McLeods' shared passion, and the pair went back to Africa often. In November of 2015, the couple returned to Jinja, this time with one-way tickets and big plans: they were going to adopt a child themselves, a process they knew could take years.

Uganda was a British colony until 1962, giving the country a unique blend of traditional African culture, with its mud huts and grass roofs, and the amenities of Western culture. "Many Americans are always surprised to find most homes in Jinja have electricity and running water," Mary says. "To be honest, I was surprised too! It's a very westernized town and most people speak English." According to Mary, it's not only the culture that surprises visitors, but the landscape and climate as well. "Many people think Uganda is really hot and desert-like," she explains, "but in fact, it's very green and has the most beautiful mixture of humidity and dryness. I always say it's like California and Florida had a baby and made Uganda. For me, it's the perfect blend of both."

While wading through mounds of bureaucratic paperwork and enduring the anguish of canceled court dates, Mary and JP settled into their new lifestyle and welcomed a biological daughter while they waited for their elder daughter's adoption to be finalized. On a typical weekday afternoon, their youngest would wait for the school bus to drop off the oldest. "Then we would all play outside, make dinner, and enjoy it on the front steps of our house until the sun went down. On the weekends, we would sleep in, make

pancakes, go to the farmer's market, and have movie nights or hang out with friends." It wasn't long until Uganda became the family's home. "Most of the time, living in Jinja felt really normal to us. But of course, there were times when we could definitely feel that we were living abroad—like when the power would go off for weeks at a time, or when we found bats living in our roof, or, most often, when we had to go to seven different supermarkets just to find an elusive ingredient that we needed for a favorite recipe."

Years of waiting in a foreign country meant that Mary and JP's relationship with each other and with their girls was more important than ever. "We learned to put our family first and focus on our handful of friendships that we could dive deep with," says Mary. "The small community that we became a part of would have gone to the ends of the world for us. Dropping off meals on hard days, stopping by the clinic to pray over our sick child, watching our kids when we just needed an adult getaway, or bringing items from the States when they had extra room in their luggage. We grew to appreciate the small gifts of life."

Those small gifts meant all the more as the waiting stretched into years. But Mary took what could have been idle time and channeled it into a productive outlet that married her love of creativity with the skills of her newfound community. "We were faced with long seasons filled with little answers," she says. "I needed an outlet, and thankfully I knew incredible, local artisans

"What started as a temporary stay overseas has become another home for us, filled with memories of green forests, misty mornings, and dear friends."

The landscape diversity of Uganda is unique with its lush rolling hills, forests, waterfalls, lakes, snowcapped mountains, rivers, and vast tracks of savannah grasslands.

“We learned to put our family first and focus on a handful of friendships that we could dive deep with. The small community that we became a part of would have gone to the ends of the world for us.”

In April 2019, nearly four years after the process began, the McLeods' adoption was officially finalized. Later that year, they returned to California to start a new chapter of life as a family of four.

"I imagine that we will grow old with these people; we'll always have crazy memories and stories to talk about together, and we know for sure that we can always rely on each other, no matter how many miles separate us."

who could help bring to life the designs that were floating around in my mind. We began making designs and building inventory while in Uganda, eventually launching a little Etsy shop called Atlas Skye, in honor of our baby that we miscarried in Uganda." Mary's Etsy shop sells custom-designed handmade goods, supporting Ugandan employees in the process. "We established incredible relationships with the artisans that have continued even after we eventually moved back to the States."

In April 2019, nearly four years after the process began, the McLeods' adoption was officially finalized. Later that year, they returned to California to start a new chapter of life as a family of four. Forever grateful for the time they spent living in Africa and the lifelong friendships they made there, the family hopes to continue making a positive impact in the community that was, for years, their home. "Being able to help support families in Uganda through Atlas Skye has been such a blessing and it has grown into something way bigger than I ever imagined," says Mary. "What started as a temporary stay overseas has become another home for us, filled with memories of green forests, misty mornings, and dear friends. Our family began in Uganda, and for the last four years, it is all we have known. Now that we're living in the States, we realize that there are things that our community here will never understand, so this sense of unity has grown even stronger with our community back in Uganda. I imagine that we will grow old with these people; we'll always have crazy memories and stories to talk about together, and we know for sure that we can always rely on each other, no matter how many miles happen to separate us."

From the Cold North to the Land of the Rising Sun

FINLAND AND JAPAN

JOPSU AND TIMO RAMU, MIMI (9), MUUSA (6), VILI (4), AND IGGY (1.5)

A family of creative nomads split their time between Finland and Japan and embrace the best of life in both cultures.

The Ramu family is most at home when they're on the move. "Traveling means everything for our family and for our work. It's where we get our inspiration and it's what makes us happy," says Jopsu Ramu. "We love driving a Defender over tough conditions around Iceland or Norway, we don't mind getting our hands dirty at a vanilla farm in French Polynesia, and we love surfing with our friends down in Byron Bay."

Together with her husband Timo, Jopsu is the co-founder of Musuta, an award-winning, multidisciplinary studio that produces film, animation, art, and design projects for clients such as New Balance, Muji, the James Bond franchise, Star Alliance, and Nokia. With their shared love of adventure and a growing portfolio of global collaborators, the Ramus happily embrace any chance they get to travel the globe. "Because of the remote nature of our work, most of the time, nobody cares exactly *where* we are in the world," Jopsu explains, "so we can usually be wherever we want to be."

For the past decade, the two places that Jopsu, Timo, and their four children have wanted to be most are their home country of Finland and the sprawling megalopolis of Tokyo. The family's connection with Japan goes back more than 20 years, to the time Jopsu spent there as an exchange student in high school. Later, she and Timo began traveling to Japan together for extended periods,

“When we’re in Helsinki, life is so well organized for families,” says Jopsu Ramu. “It’s very safe, the schools are world-famous, we’re always close to nature, and it’s easy to find quiet.”

For the Ramus, travel is the ultimate form of curiosity. But there is another dimension to the family's passion for adventure: "Every time you travel, you're traveling within yourself—growing, changing, and expanding," explains Jopsu.

"It is very enriching to live in both places," says Jopsu Ramu. "Our kids have come to understand that the people of the world often look, behave, and think differently. They have friends in both countries, and they happily call both places home."

"We feel privileged to live in this way, but it's not one continuous holiday: we suffer from jet lag, kids get sick, we need to be careful with finances, and we have to try to maintain a healthy balance for our children."

backpacking through the country, studying the language, and taking university classes. "There is something in Japanese aesthetics, architecture, design, and culture that has always drawn us back," says Jopsu. "Eventually, we started to make really close friends and working relationships in the country." The couple was spending more and more time in Japan for work, often collaborating with local creative partners. "In 2010, along with one of our Japanese colleagues, we won a Gold Lion in Cannes, which was really meaningful for us," says Jopsu. That same year, the Ramus decided it was time to set up a studio in Tokyo and begin splitting their time more equitably between Finland and Japan. "We had been going back and forth constantly," Jopsu says, "so it just made sense for us to establish a base, so we could feel at home in both places."

A decade later, the Ramus are convinced the arrangement suits their family perfectly. All four of their kids were born into this dynamic lifestyle, so the transition from one nation to the other is more or less natural for the whole family. "It is very enriching to live in both places," Jopsu says. "Our kids have come to understand that the people of the world often look, behave, and think differently. They have friends in both countries and they happily call both places home."

For the Ramus, Japan and Finland are equally inspiring places. "When we're in Helsinki, life is so well organized for families," Jopsu says. "It's very safe, the schools are world-famous, we're always close to nature, and it's easy to find quiet." By contrast, Tokyo is exciting and educational in other ways: "It has this big, bustling energy and yet, it's still such a clean, safe, and orderly city." A typical day out for the family in Finland might include a walk in the woods, a day of boating, or an afternoon at the sauna. In Tokyo, they spend their free time wandering farmers' markets, visiting museums, and picnicking in one of the city's many parks. But there are downsides to having dual homes, as Jopsu is quick to note: "We feel privileged to live in this way, but it's not one continuous holiday: we still suffer from jet lag, kids get sick, we need to be careful with finances, and we also have to try to maintain a healthy balance of fun and stability for our children."

In order to make their unique lifestyle work, the Ramus have several family principles: keep expectations flexible (especially while traveling), separate work and family time, and stick to routines, which act as an anchor no matter where they are in the world. "Because our lives are ever-changing, routines are crucial," says Jopsu. "We realized that the best way to get our work done was to wake up super early and work before the kids get up. Then we can fill the gaps of nap times with work—and so manage to put in a full day's work while still keeping it separate from family time."

For the Ramus, travel is the ultimate form of curiosity. But there is another dimension to the family's passion for adventure: "Every time you travel, you're traveling within yourself—growing, changing, and expanding," explains Jopsu. "When we go outside our safe, familiar surroundings, we are forced to adapt, learn new skills, and rediscover who we really are." By raising their family in two very different cultures, Jopsu and Timo hope they are passing on this legacy of self-discovery, curiosity, and empathy to their children. "Our kids were born into a family that loves to travel," Jopsu says. "It will be really exciting to see how this impacts them as they grow up."

Explore More

SO, YOU WANNA EXPATRIATE?
Living, working, and raising kids in another country can be a fascinating, enlightening, and life-changing experience for a family. But moving your family abroad is not always easy to do.

START WITH YOUR (NET)WORK
Usually, the simplest way to live abroad, legally, is through study or work. Lots of online resources provide links to international job opportunities, expatriate groups, and tips on how to make it work.

PARLEZ-VOUS FRANÇAIS?
If you want to go abroad for work, then the places you will be able to move will likely (though not always), be limited by the language(s) you can speak. So, start brushing up those Mandarin skills.

START THE CONVERSATION
While moving abroad is always exciting, it can be tough for the whole family. Start talking openly and honestly with the kids early on about the benefits and challenges of possibly moving abroad.

FULL DISCLOSURE
Ask any parent who has moved their family abroad and they will tell you: culture shock is real, language barriers can be intense, and kids, especially, can often feel unmoored by so much change.

TRAVEL TIPS: SEVEN TO TEN

Limitations to travel drastically fall away once children reach the ages from seven to ten. They can entertain themselves, handle bathrooms on their own, and even carry some of their own luggage. Now that they do not need to nap, your schedule can incorporate many more possibilities, and the fact that you no longer need to carry a universe of child-related stuff with you means you can be much more flexible. Perhaps most importantly of all, kids in this age group have not yet developed the embarrassing-parent complex—that tendency to look away and roll their eyes when mom or dad do something "cringey." Instead, you might find in your child a willing travel buddy who gets enjoyment out of the same things you do.

Choosing a Destination

There is a vast range of destinations suitable for children of elementary school ages, and by this time they can be involved in the decision-making. Child-friendly cruises are delightful experiences, often including entertainment such as surfing simulators, bumper cars, water parks, and bowling alleys. Camping in the great outdoors is another fantastic option, with some campsites providing specialized facilities for those traveling with children.

Settings like these can help kids learn how to socialize outside of their usual circles. For day trips or pit stops, adventure parks like Legoland are not only immense fun, but can also be deployed as a compromise for whatever boring activity you have inflicted on your child beforehand.

How to Get There

The beauty of a cruise is that it's both a mode of transportation and an experience in itself. Generally speaking, ships headed to the Caribbean or the Mediterraneans have a good range of child-friendly options. Newer vessels are always preferable—they have often been designed with kids in mind. Getting to a destination by road, air, or rail is of course a more direct way to travel, if you're under time constraints. In such cases, aim to book nighttime journeys, especially if they are long haul, to help eliminate inevitable restlessness. Whatever the mode of transportation, have kids look after their own bags in transit—it's a great way for them to learn how to be responsible travelers.

Checklist (For a Cruise)

- Travel documents (passports, reservation information, insurance)
- Proof of purchase for pre-booked land activities
- Daytime clothes (one set for each day, plus spares)
- Rain jackets, sunglasses, and hats
- Clothing options for dinner
- Sandals and covered shoes (including hiking footwear if required)
- Bathing suits (at least two different options)
- Towels and Water bottles
- Snorkel gear (including flippers) and Boogie boards
- Electronic devices (tablets, phones, headphones, laptops, chargers, memory cards)
- Waterproof cases for electronics (lanyard-style for phones)
- Lanyard cases for key cards
- Multi plug adapter and batteries
- Notebooks and travel journals
- Waterproof camera (electronic or disposable)
- Sunscreen, insect repellant, seasickness tablets
- First aid kit and antihistamines
- Laundry detergent

Where to Sleep

Cruise ships have a variety of rooms that cater to the needs of families. Known as cruise rooms, staterooms, or cabins,

these accommodations typically sleep four to five people, but there are often options available that can host up to ten. Cabins like these are divided internally by either solid walls or blackout curtains, allowing for privacy or quiet time, and comprise a mix of movable beds, foldout sofas, or pullout sleeping units. If you can't fit everyone in one room, try to book adjacent cabins so you are near each other. For land journeys, many hotels class children in this age group as minors and do not charge for their stays. The Ibis hotel group, for example, is a budget option that offers free accommodations and breakfast for up to two children under 16 if they're sharing their parents' room.

Where to Eat

Elementary school children will be able to contribute when it comes to choosing a place to eat, and, depending on the child, they may even have strong preferences. While it is important to allow kids of this age some say in where you go, setting limits and being a good example will hopefully nudge them down a healthy path. In restaurants, introduce children to the culinary variety found when traveling by getting them to try some of your appetizer or main. This will help to broaden their palates and get them familiar with unusual cuisines. Sticking to regular eating times is also an important part of keeping children happy while on a trip, so be sure to have substantial snacks handy if a regular mealtime is out of the question.

How to Move Around

Navigating cities can be an exciting experience for kids in this age group. They may already be familiar with transport systems in their hometown, so seeing the way they work somewhere else provides a mind-broadening source of contrast and comparison, and an opportunity to expand their orienteering skills. Show them when and where you plan to go with maps of underground train networks and bus and tram schedules. Once you're on your way, track your trip's progress with them by taking note of the stations or stops as you pass by. See if they can figure out where they are or where to get off; you can make this easier for younger children by counting down the stops before your final destination.

Unexpected Twists

Allergies are important to keep in mind when traveling. The most common food allergies result from milk, eggs, wheat, soy, and nuts, and will therefore already be known to parents with children in this age group, but trying new foods for the first time, especially seafood, may produce an entirely new allergic reaction. Symptoms can include vomiting, diarrhea, swelling, cramps, rashes, and, in serious cases, breathing difficulties. Knowing these symptoms and the emergency services' phone number in your destination are absolute necessities. Other kinds of reactions can occur from exposure to new environments, specifically from dust, pollen, mold, and animals, so bring along some antihistamines just in case.

Hack

Car or seasickness can't always be avoided. After all, you have to move around when you travel, so the best you can do is learn to manage this kind of illness—and hope it doesn't occur on a two-week cruise. Activities that really bring on motion sickness are reading or looking at a fixed point inside a moving vehicle, so get children to look outside while you are in motion. You can make this more fun by turning it into a game—I Spy is a perfect solution for car or boat trips. There are two main versions: one takes letters as its prompt—"I spy with my little eye something beginning with A"—and the other puts colors in place of letters. Alternatively, listen to audiobooks while the affected child looks out the window.

Shared Journeys along the Legendary Silk Road

INDIA

RACHEL AND GAWAINE GLASBY, LUNA INDIGO (4) AND ZAALA ZAHARA (2)

A lifelong traveler shares her love of India by helping other women experience the country's endless wonders.

For nearly 2,000 years, the Silk Road thrived as a vast network of trade routes responsible for connecting the cultures, customs, and commodities of the East and West. Today the Silk Road has taken on a new life, attracting travelers from all over the world to vibrant cities touched by centuries of humanity. But, for women traveling solo to these historic destinations, there are considerable unknowns around personal safety that deter many from ever making the voyage.

This reality inspired Rachel Glasby to found *The Silk Road,* a socially-minded online platform that offers women the opportunity to join expertly guided trips to India, hosted by Rachel herself. *The Silk Road* began as a webshop where Rachel could sell handmade objects she was collecting on her family's travels through India, Iran, Turkey, and Morocco. Today it has evolved into a multi-faceted digital space where Rachel shares her travel photography, information on her work collaborating with NGOs and Fair Trade Organisations, and invites other women to join her on adventurous trips into the subcontinent.

Originally from North Queensland, Australia, Rachel grew up in the lush rain forests and mountains tucked along the tropical seaboard. Today, she lives in Adelaide with her husband Gawaine and daughters Luna Indigo and Zaala Zahara. But throughout her

For nearly 2,000 years, the Silk Road thrived as a vast network of trade routes responsible for connecting the cultures, customs, and commodities of the East and West. Today the Silk Road has taken on a new life, attracting travelers from all over the world.

“I believe that travel can be a powerful way to expand our understanding of the world and humanity beyond the life we were raised in,” says Rachel Glasby, “quite simply, it gives you a fuller picture of the world.”

"I hope our own children come to understand that people of different backgrounds and beliefs make up a beautiful collection of loving and peaceful humans," says Rachel Glasby. "We all have more similarities than differences."

"After a few days, my senses began to align with what was happening around me and an easy flow set in. The world around me, although bustling with a frenetic energy as only India can, began to slow down."

life, she has made countless trips to India, getting acquainted with a country that has become a second home. "After a decade of regular visits, I feel a sense of comfort and ease as I navigate streets I once found overwhelming," she says. "The density, noise, and raw energy are all still there, but now I better understand it, and I love it." Spending time in India with her daughters has had a powerful impact and made Rachel want to share these journeys with others. "I know how easy and rewarding it can be with a little planning. I also understand that for many, exploring India independently with your children is a total leap of faith into uncharted territory."

Rachel describes the understandable culture shock that many face when visiting a country as vast and daunting as India. "I can remember feeling overwhelmed just by stepping onto the street," she recalls. "A sea of car horns blaring, bright yellow and green auto-rickshaws darting past, cows meandering, and so many people everywhere. But, over time, a comfortable sense of India emerges." As her travels became more frequent, Rachel's once-reluctant friends started asking if they could join her. She realized that she could help relieve the hesitancy of uncertain travelers and fuel their curiosity as a source of trust. "I decided to help them navigate through my own experience," she says.

By focusing on sharing travels as a bonded group of mothers, Rachel has confidently guided visitors past the tourist traps and deeper into everyday life in India. "One of my favorite memories is a sunrise hike we took to a temple set in the hills outside of Jaipur," she says. "We ventured up the mountain and past the usual tourist photo stop until we came across a spring. There we were greeted by a group of women singing in the water. They welcomed us with open arms and within a few minutes, we were in the water alongside them laughing and splashing. It was such a stunning reminder that motherhood and sisterhood can always transcend religion or culture."

As a visitor in India, Rachel is keenly aware of the need to balance her role as an outsider, a guide, and a mother. "I would like to dispel the idea that traveling in India with kids is an unusual achievement," she says. "The reality is there are millions of mothers going about their lives with children every single day in India. I have no secret skills that allow me to explore India with my children and I would be showing Indian women great disrespect by suggesting otherwise." Rachel's candor in honoring the country most clearly manifests in her dedication to supporting its people and their labors. "After years of rummaging through the bazaars, markets, souks, and chowks along the trade routes of the original Silk Road, I had a realization: the inspiration I found and my love of meeting artisans led me to want to share their beautiful art with my community in Australia. Over time this has grown and we have now sent pieces all over the world, to New York, Tokyo, Rio, and Paris." Rachel now collaborates with artisans, international NGOs, and fair trade groups that support local women's initiatives. "Weaving conscious consumerism into the travel experiences helps support artisans with a fair wage and working conditions that ensure safety, health, and dignity for the community," she says.

Looking back, Rachel can see the profound effect that traveling through India has had on both herself and her daughters. "It teaches us empathy and a deeper understanding that people of different backgrounds and beliefs make up the collective beauty of humanity. Quite simply, it gives us a fuller picture of the world." Her hope for the future is to continue exploring India's enchanting nature and vibrant cities, sharing unforgettable moments with other mothers and children ready to experience more of the beauty that the world has to offer.

Explore More

INTO THE SUBCONTINENT

India is the seventh-largest country in the world and the second-most populous.The country is a busy, complex tapestry of cultures. Before traveling there, do your homework. Here's a brief introduction …

THE NORTH

This region includes the cities of New Delhi, Agra, and Jaipur, the Taj Mahal, the Thar Desert, and Ranthambore National Park. The rainy season here lasts from May to September, so try to visit from October to April.

THE SOUTH

Key southern cities and sights include: the beaches of Kerala, colonial Pondicherry, Periyar National Park, Parambikulam Tiger Reserve, the surreal Meenakshi Amman Temple, and the Chithirai Festival.

THE WEST

This region includes the states of Goa, Gujarat, and Maharashtra, bustling Mumbai, the stunning Ellora Caves, and Tadoba and Navegaon National Parks. The best time to visit is from November to February.

THE BEST OF THE REST

In the east, Darjeeling and Kolkata are essential stops. In the northeast, Guwahati is a good base for exploring the state of Assam. In central India, visit the Mahabodhi Temple Complex, where Buddhism was born.

What We Carried Home: Two Years of Travel, Discovery, and Friendship

A family leaves behind their home in Seattle in order to travel around the world for 24 months, with hopes of experiencing a great adventure and gaining an appreciation for what domestic life looks like in other cultures.

MARTIN PENNER AND TARYN ELLEDGE-PENNER, MATILDA (9), FRANCIS (7), AND VIGGO (4)

It was nearing midnight in Tokyo. Martin Penner and Taryn Elledge-Penner, surrounded by their three jet-lagged children and a pile of luggage, stared up at a map inside Shinjuku station—the busiest train station in the world—wondering how to get "home," and what it would look like when they got there. Later that night, the family of five found their way to a friend's place in Tokyo's Nerima district, and home turned out to be a late-night bowl of ramen, soft beds rolled out on the floor, and dreams of the next day's adventures.

A year earlier, Martin and Taryn had sold nearly everything they had, packed what they could and left their home in Seattle for an around-the-world adventure. Together with their kids Matilda, Francis, and Viggo, they started traveling full-time with hopes of experiencing what family life looks like in other cultures. By the time they arrived in Japan in May 2019, they had already journeyed through Europe, Africa, and Asia and had long since left the edge of the map they'd imagined when they boarded a one-way flight to Paris 11 months earlier.

Martin and Taryn grew up in small communities on opposite sides of the Canada-U.S. border. They met in 2006, and it wasn't long before they were traveling together to places they'd always dreamed about: Paris, Rome, Marrakech, Jerusalem, and far-flung Ouagadougou. Their first baby, Matilda, arrived while the pair was working in Paris—she was born just off the Place de la République while Parisians outside chanted for a better tomorrow. By the time the family returned to Seattle, they knew someday they'd be back out on the road.

Life in Seattle was filled with good friends, interesting work, and the clean water and deep forests of the Pacific Northwest. "We knew we were leaving something special," says Martin. "But we wanted our kids to know the grandness of the world, to see and feel things that inspired them and, just as importantly, made them uncomfortable in some way. We wanted to turn them upside down, shake a bit, and see how different the world looked when we set them back on their feet."

Paris, full of friends and memories, was an easy first stop. From there, the family's path was guided by research needs for Quartier Collective, a boutique travel agency for curious families the couple had created on the eve of their departure. Italy, Greece, Portugal, Spain, Ireland, Morocco, Sri Lanka, Japan, and Australasia—in 20 months, the family put 15 stamps in their passports, with stays as short as a week and as long as three months. In Greece and Morocco, Martin and Taryn produced special events called Family Gatherings, which brought small groups of families

Martin Penner and his son Viggo, watching the sunrise over a palm grove in Skoura, Morocco in December 2018. "Here, we spent our days walking in the palms and chasing running streams, and our evenings making Christmas presents for each other."

> "We knew we were leaving something special back home, but we wanted our kids to know the grandness of the world, to see and feel things that inspired them and, just as importantly, made them uncomfortable in some way."

together for a week of discovery, good food, and adventure. They describe their approach as "traveling to find people, not places," and though children make travel more complicated, they've found that having kids along for the journey changes the experience for everybody. "In many parts of the world, children are a key that opens the door to homes, cultures, and new friends," says Martin. "Our family was welcomed warmly in the same streets that felt cold and even unsettling as a solo traveler."

When asked about their favorite destination during the two-year voyage abroad, the entire family gives the same answer: Japan. "Japan is everything we'd hoped and so much we couldn't have imagined," says Martin. "It's like living in a shiny future, singing toilets included, with a deep care for things that are old or slow, plus the best food in the world." The two months the family spent there were a balance between the rushing blur of the cities and the serenity of the countryside. For three weeks, they stayed at the hobby farm of an eccentric Japanese art collector—an ancient wooden machiya house filled with curiosities in the bottom of a green valley. The farm had a cafe attached, open three days a week with as many items on the menu and perfect coffee. Strange and fascinating people regularly stopped by; the big tatami room would swell with futons for those who stayed overnight—filmmakers, a hipster farmer who brought live chickens for dinner, a sake maker, a Tokyo hip hop artist, and an old neighbor carrying

a bottomless bottle of Suntory whisky and a 10-meter (33-feet) length of bamboo that became a slide for a soba-noodle party. "We all grabbed a spot along the bamboo," remembers Martin. "The noodles, carried by a stream of water from the garden hose, came rushing by and we stabbed frantically with our chopsticks till our bellies hurt from laughter and soba. The next morning Viggo used the bamboo as a chute for his toy cars. We still talk about that evening—whenever we have a bowl of noodles, we wish we were eating from a bamboo slide."

For more than two years, the ground under their feet was constantly moving. And yet, Martin, Taryn, and their globe-trotting kids were able to establish patterns of communication, rest, intimacy, and shared memory-making that organically evolved into a new kind of home away from home. "During that period, the logistics of life were more complicated than ever," says Martin, "but the things that are most important to our family remained front and center. We had no room for souvenirs, so what we carried home, in the end, were memories of this unique chapter; we have the priceless time that we spent together, and the countless experiences and new relationships that continue to inspire us today." While the start of their journey relied on a shared tolerance for risk, the ensuing two years demanded substantial growth from each member of the family. This is where, for Martin and Taryn, travel's greatest value lies. "We've seen in our kids, in each other, and in the friends we've made along the way, that there is no better way to develop an adaptable and creative mindset—one able to approach our world's biggest issues and our own search for happiness—than through curious, open-hearted, and respectful travel."

"In many parts of the world, children are a key that opens the door to homes, cultures, and new friends. Our family was welcomed warmly in the same streets that felt cold and even unsettling as a solo traveler."

Martin and Viggo Penner photographed at Kasbah Bab Ourika in Ourika, Morocco in October 2019. The Kasbah is a citadel-like castle perched on a steep knoll overlooking the lush Ourika valley below and Morocco's High Atlas Mountains in the distance.

Matilda Penner at play on the beach in Ahangama, Sri Lanka, February 2019. "The southern coast of Sri Lanka has heavy swells that time of year," her dad says, "and while the surfing was amazing, swimming for the kids was done with plenty of caution."

“We had no room for souvenirs, so what we carried home in the end were memories; we have the priceless time that we spent together, and the countless experiences and new relationships that continue to inspire us today.”

Where the River Meets the Sea: A Holiday Refuge Where Life Moves Slower

FFOREST FARM, NEAR CARDIGAN (WALES, UK)

EMMA AND JAMES DONNELLY, MONTY (14) AND AGNES (12)

Each year, a busy family returns to the idyllic Welsh countryside to unplug from the noise and hit the reset button.

There are so many wonderful places around the world worth visiting for one's precious family holidays. So, it says volumes about a place when a family returns, time and again, year after year. Happy memories can become deeply rooted in such locations; the familiar sights, sounds, and smells of a favorite place weaving together with the new memories made on each return visit. The Swedes have a name for this sort of special place: a *smultronställe,* or "wild strawberry patch," a place of comfort and refuge, worth traveling to again and again, both physically and in memory.

For Emma and James Donnelly, their family's "wild strawberry patch" is fforest, a historic 81-hectare (200-acre) farm turned nature retreat in idyllic western Wales. "It's a place where we can relax and live outside day and night," Emma says. "Our kids always make new friends there and they can basically just roam free; there is easy access to both the river and the sea, and the area has an abundance of wildlife. We've been drawn back almost every year, and it's the place that helps our family hit the reset button."

Located alongside the River Teifi, just inland from the wide beaches and hidden coves that look out over the Irish Sea, fforest was established in 2004, as a place to enjoy the simplicity, pleasures, and beauty of outdoor living. Its founders describe it as

TYPHOON

“Sleeping outside under canvas, looking up at the stars overhead, listening to the owls in the trees and the rustle of creatures in the hedgerows, this is a big part of what makes this place so special.”

Located alongside the River Teifi, just inland from the wide beaches and hidden coves that look out over the Irish Sea, fforest farm was established in 2004, as a place to enjoy the simplicity, pleasures, and beauty of outdoor living.

“Sleeping outside under canvas,” says Emma Donnelly, “looking up at the stars overhead, listening to the owls in the trees and the rustle of creatures in the hedgerows, this is a big part of what makes this place so special.”

For the Donnelly family, time spent at fforest is more than just a nice change of pace. “It’s such a time of freedom for all of us,” Emma says, “showering, cooking, and playing outside all day is incredibly calming and it bonds us together.”

"It is a place where their family has grown up making memories together—a place as familiar as an old friend, as refreshing as a river swim, and as comforting as the warm glow of a campfire."

"the result of a dream—the dream of trying to remember what 'simple' can look, feel, and taste like."

Emma first discovered fforest several years ago, while thumbing through a travel magazine. "I read that the founders, Sian and James—who have since become friends—had left London with their four sons to create a new, simpler way of life that they could also share with others," Emma explains. "So, they renovated a big Georgian farmhouse, built some new cabins warmed by log-burning stoves, and established their own little pub on-site." Along with beach and river access, Emma learned that fforest offers a diverse range of opportunities for being outdoors day and night, "from exploring the local marshes to working in the vegetable garden and gathering together around the fire for good food and wine each evening." For Emma and James—who both work in the fast-paced creative industry—it sounded like the perfect place for their young family to unwind together and make some new memories.

Each journey west to fforest is a chance for the Donnellys to slow down and refocus on what is most important. "The pace of life in Wales is so beautifully slow," says Emma. "The nature unfurls around you and it's all just so absolutely stunning; we have so many beautiful memories from the times we've spent there." After a long drive from their home in Leigh-on-Sea, east of London, the family makes the final approach to their holiday home on foot. "Everyone is asked to park their car at the bottom of a hill and walk up to the lodge," Emma explains. "This five-minute walk is important to help you begin your time at fforest, to be inspired by the magical setting, and to adjust to the pace of the farm." As the family ascends the hill, the friendly scent of woodsmoke greets them first. "You can always smell woodsmoke at fforest," Emma explains. "There are several outdoor fire pits around the property as well as log burners in every cabin and dome, and in the beautiful little pub." After leaving the cares of home, the busy motorway, and the car far behind, it's time for the family to get reacquainted with their favorite place. "The first thing you do when you arrive is meet with one of the lovely staff, sit by the fire on Welsh blankets, share a pot of tea together and have a little chat," says Emma. Within a matter of minutes, mom and dad are fully relaxed while the kids are off roaming with newfound friends, "like a pack of feral animals, exploring the woods with sticks in hand and their imaginations running wild." At night, the family's immersion into the full holiday experience is completed, as they fall asleep in one of fforest's cozy canvas domes. "Sleeping outside under canvas," Emma says, "looking up at the stars overhead, listening to the owls in the trees and the rustle of creatures in the hedgerows, this is a big part of what makes this place so special."

For the Donnellys, time spent at fforest is more than just a nice change of pace. "It's such a time of freedom for all of us," Emma says, "showering, cooking, and playing outside all day is incredibly calming and it bonds us together." Whether they spend their days dolphin-watching on the beach, canoeing down the river, or visiting the farmer's markets in the nearby village of St. Dogmaels, this quiet little corner of Wales is the spot where the Donnelly family knows they can both relax and be inspired by a slower, simpler way of life. It is a place where their family has grown up making memories together—a place as familiar as an old friend, as refreshing as a river swim, and as comforting as the warm glow of a campfire.

Explore More

WELCOME TO WALES

Wales is a small (just three million people live there), green, and serene country home to rugged coastlines, enchanting forests, friendly folks, and more castles per square mile than any other European country.

GET YOUR (SCENIC) STEPS IN

There are more than 2,200 kilometers (1,300 miles) of public walking/hiking paths crisscrossing Wales' incredible landscapes. The trails vary in difficulty but most are dotted with charming towns and villages.

RACE YOU TO THE TOP

Wales has three national parks which cover roughly 20 percent of the country's land area. The nation's highest peak is Snowdon—located in Snowdonia National Park—which rises to a hikable height of 1,085 meters (3,560 feet).

TRY COASTEERING

Coasteering is a unique, active way to experience the dramatic Welsh coastline. Guided tours include cave exploration, cliff jumping, and "adventure swimming" for kids (aged 8+) and adults alike.

REQUIRED READING

The author Roald Dahl was born in Wales and his fantastical books continue to delight kids of all ages. Grown-ups will do well to revisit the timeless works of Dylan Thomas, Wales' most famous writer.

Never the Same Path Twice

By Reif Larsen

In the before times, I used to travel a lot with my kids. When my first child, Holt, was two, we split our time between Scotland and Upstate New York, and so we grew adept at navigating the various perils of transatlantic flights with young ones in tow. When I look back on it now, I see that we were often *traveling*—where you are moving through space and time—but not always *journeying*—where your mind is alight with measuring the distance between here and there.

Like billions of others during the Covid-19 pandemic, our family has not been traveling anywhere. Our world has shrunk considerably. We've all been forced to recalibrate our coordinates, to rethink the possibilities of space, to seek out journeys closer to home.

During the early days of the pandemic, I found it essential to take a daily walk. Routine can be a balm in times of great uncertainty. My walks coincided with the discovery of a trail right near my house in Troy, NY, that began at the edge of a cemetery and descended through a forest to the meandering bends of the Poestenkill River.

What wonder! And so close to home. Stumbling upon the path felt like I had found a wormhole, a portal to another world, at once so near and so far from our doorstep. The world could be burning and this place would not know. Or perhaps this place had known all along.

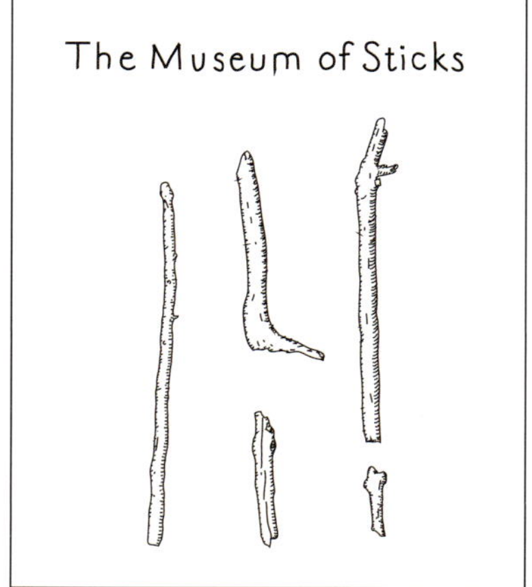

I discovered the path in early spring, when the trees were still bare. At the time, I was listening to *War and Peace* on audiobook and the regularity of the narrative—the walk, the words, the trees—was one of my few daily comforts. I walked the path every day, listening to Prussian battlefields and Moscow drawing-room drama, marveling at the forest's gentle metamorphosis into spring, buds bursting forth like fireworks in slow motion. Following the same path again and again felt life affirming, a kind of heartbeat in transit.

I wanted to share this place with my children. I wasn't quite sure how they would react to the path that had become so important to me. I was a little bit nervous about breaking the serenity of such hallowed ground. But everything must be broken eventually.

"Where are we going?" asked Holt, now six. He and his brother Max, three, had spent much of their time distance-learning on screens during the quarantine, and so I was always trying to herd them outside. I didn't want them to forget the feeling of sunlight on their faces.

"To the river," I said.

I needn't have worried about breaking the serenity of my path—it was broken within seconds.

"Did you know that Achilles has a great weakness?" said Holt, swinging a stick at a tree trunk that was bent a bit like an ankle.

"Where's my lightsaber?"

said Max, searching for his lost stick-cum-Jedi-weapon.

If you've ever tried to get anywhere with young children, you know it is a meandering affair. There are many stops. Many questions. Hooks cast out into the ether.

"Did you know there's a *real* Mount Olympus?" said Holt.

"Does it look like this?" I said, gesturing at the forest.

Holt looked around, considering for a long moment, "No, it's got temples and there's fire everywhere."

We paused, ruminating on the lack of temples in these parts. Or the fact that there were temples everywhere. I pointed out a frenetic robin who had returned early, perhaps, to survey the damage. To start a family. Or to simply give up.

We stooped and examined a busy ant colony. I told them that ants didn't talk with words but with scents.

"Everything is so smelly for ants!" said Max.

We walked down the path a little further, searching for good sticks. My sons had become stick connoisseurs. This one was a crossbow; this one was a tennis racket; this one was a gearshift; this one was a staff; this one was a telescope. Our garage had been turned into a museum of sticks.

"What do you see?" I asked Holt as he stared through a telescope stick.

"Oh, Maxi …" said Holt. "Here comes Zeus!"

Would we be better off in the Louvre? On the rim of the Grand Canyon? Wandering through the favelas of Rio? For these two, I'm not sure. Travels abound.

"Lightning!" said Max and ducked, but lazily, to indicate that he was only ducking for our amusement.

Would we ever travel abroad again? In a warming, pandemic-filled world, *should* we travel again? If my sons never ventured much further than this path, what kind of people would they grow up to be? Was travel necessary to cultivate empathy, understanding, perspective? One could travel without journeying. Could one journey without traveling?

We walked further into the woods. From high above our heads, a woodpecker clapped out a short staccato, plucking for insects. Max picked up a stick and a stone.

"Turn around, Daddy," he said. "Tell me if this is a stone or a real woodpecker."

– toc toc toc toc –

"A real woodpecker," I said.

"No, it was me!" said Max.

We reached the river's edge. It was running high from recent spring rains. The water churned and gurgled on its way to the eventual sea. Never the same river twice.

We ambled down to a little pebble beach. I found a perfectly flat stone and skipped it, in one hop, to the other side.

"This is our kitchen," Holt announced, stacking rocks into an oven. "We're making pizzas. This is Italy."

We made delicious, succulent stone pizzas by the riverside. Our toppings drifted into the fantastic: car parts, dragon's teeth, precious gems. If only we could make a cookbook to capture such marvels.

I've since taken Max and Holt on the same path down to the river. Spring has now sprung. The woods have become new woods entirely. The ground is thick with vegetation, a rich pageantry of tangled growth. We can no longer see what comes around the next bend. The air is filled with a symphony of bird song. The solitary robin is surrounded by his kin.

On a recent walk, Max was momentarily confused at such transformation. He tapped his stick on the path.

"Is this the same place as before?" he asked.

"Of course it is," said Holt.

"I'm not so sure," I said and started walking again.

REIF LARSEN is author of the novels The Selected Works of T. S. Spivet *and* I Am Radar.

Into the Woods and Far from the Maddening Crowds

FORESTS AROUND BERLIN, GERMANY

ANNA LIVSIC AND JIL (4)

A family escapes the hustle and bustle of Berlin in search of peace, quiet, and wild mushrooms.

Anna Livsic lives in the heart of Berlin, Germany. A growing center of commercial activity, the area has the surroundings to match: neatly paved roads, multistory concrete buildings, and small parks dotted here and there. The unceasing daily hubbub that fills the air may feel natural to some, but for Anna, urban life is a "contradiction." She feels most at home in nature, and the same goes for her husband, Mo, and four-year-old daughter, Jil. "We try to escape the city as often as possible," Anna says, "and the forest is our favorite place."

Anna's love of nature was instilled in her as a child. Growing up in the Ukraine, she has fond memories of leaving the urban sprawl behind each summer for the countryside, where she would be free to explore meadows and rivers, woodlands and wildlife. During these holidays, her mother revealed a seemingly magical knowledge of the forest. "In my childhood, my mom taught me to forage for mushrooms, wild berries, and healing herbs," she says. "As an adult, those days have become my happy place, a kind of homeland that only exists in my memories." Keenly aware of the importance of her own early adventures, Anna is set on cultivating enchanting memories for Jil: "What I am doing with my daughter now, is sharing the same kinds of experiences that made me so happy as a kid," she says.

"Our favorite time is autumn, when mushrooms appear," says Anna Livsic. In this period, the family journeys a little further out of Berlin, to the vast meadows of Brandenburg, where, in the right conditions, the mushrooms are bountiful.

“As Jil grows, we’re better able to anticipate the challenges of traveling together; patience and good organization are still not our superpowers, but we are learning and getting better and better.”

Grunewald ("green forest") has become one of the family's favorite forests to visit. Located just 10 kilometers (6 miles) from the center of the German capital, it ranges across 3,000 hectares (7,413 acres) and consists largely of conifers and birch trees.

For Anna Livsic, urban life is a "contradiction." She, her husband Mo, and her four-year-old daughter, Jil all feel most at home in nature. "We try to escape the city as often as possible," Anna says, "and the forest is our favorite place."

"In my own childhood, my mom taught me to forage for mushrooms, wild berries, and healing herbs. What I am doing with my daughter now, is sharing the same kinds of experiences that made me so happy as a kid."

Being avid surfers, both Anna and Mo have always loved to travel, visiting coastal destinations all over Europe and Asia. When Jil was just five months old, the family took their first surf trip together, to Sri Lanka, a country prized for its sandy beaches, tropical climate, and mellow waves. That far-flung holiday, however, didn't turn out as hoped. "It was a total disaster," Anna admits. "Jil woke up every day at 4:00 a.m., and we were super tired all the time. But we kept going, and things got better and better. Now Jil is a perfect travel companion—she is funny, curious, and finally a good sleeper."

The family learned one key lesson from that early experience. "After Sri Lanka, we became more careful with our choice of travel destinations," Anna says. "As Jil grows, we're better able to anticipate the challenges of traveling together; patience and good organization are still not our superpowers, but we are learning and getting better and better."

Their forest escapes are typically spontaneous, daylong adventures that take place on the weekends and don't require much planning. The family sets out early by car and returns before dark. Grunewald ("green forest") has become one of their favorite places to visit. Just 10 kilometers (6 miles) from the center of the German capital, it ranges across 3,000 hectares (7,413 acres) and consists largely of conifers and birch trees. "The forest gives me freedom, and Jil always finds something to play with," Anna says. "It's one big natural playground—for all of us."

Having learned about the life of the forest from her mother, Anna is deeply attuned to the changing seasons. "Our favorite time is autumn, when mushrooms appear," she says. In this period, the family journeys a little further out of Berlin, to the vast meadows of Brandenburg, where, in the right conditions, the mushrooms are bountiful. "I have taught Jil to collect herbs and mushrooms, and together we observe how everything is connected in nature," she says. "It isn't always easy to convince a four-year-old to forage for mushrooms that she can't taste immediately, but she knows how the game works, how to differentiate between several types of edible and poisonous mushrooms."

Of course, venturing into the wild with a young child can involve challenges that require parents to get creative. When Jil was very small, she quickly became tired when walking long distances. So, Anna and Mo acquired a stroller with special all-terrain wheels that can smoothly traverse bumpy natural paths, knotty tree roots, and uneven beds of pine nettles. This way Jil could even nap while the family took daylong walks in the woods. Now that Jil is four, she is able to hike much longer distances and sometimes even brings her bike along to make the family's nature walks even more fun and manageable.

Much like when she was a child, Anna continues to be comforted and reenergized by her regular encounters with the beauty and harmony of nature. "After being in the forest, I feel like I'm reborn," she says, "and I have noticed that, after a day in the woods, Jil is also much more calm and balanced." Just as she inherited a love for the magical, transformative power of nature from her mother, Anna hopes a similar love will take root, blossom, and grow in her daughter's life. They plan to share many more days wandering the wild woodlands of Germany together, learning from nature, and creating lasting memories far from the clamor of the city.

Explore More

WHAT EXACTLY IS A FOREST?
Three main types of forests—tropical, temperate, and boreal—cover about 30 percent of the world's land and produce much of the oxygen we breathe. Chances are, there is a forest near you, just waiting to be explored.

ADVENTURE IN EVERY SEASON
Ask any avid hiker or woodland explorer and they'll tell you that each and every forest's "personality" changes along with the seasons, providing the opportunity for unique family experiences in the woods all year long.

ESSENTIAL GEAR
Whether you're exploring Grunewald or the woods behind your house, make sure to bring the right gear: fresh water, a mobile phone (for photos and navigation), snacks, and a pair of sturdy rubber boots.

LEARN TO FORAGE SAFELY
Wild foods are really fun to hunt for. But, before eating any wild plant or fruit, make 100 percent sure that it is safe (not poisonous). Always consult an expert, a field guide, and/or a trusty foraging app.

"BUCKET LIST" FORESTS
Arashiyama (Japan), Otzarreta Forest (Spain), Dragon's Blood Forest (Yemen), Monteverde Cloud Forest (Costa Rica), Rainbow Eucalyptus Forest (Hawaii), Black Forest (Germany), Sequoia National (USA).

TRAVEL TIPS: 11 TO 13

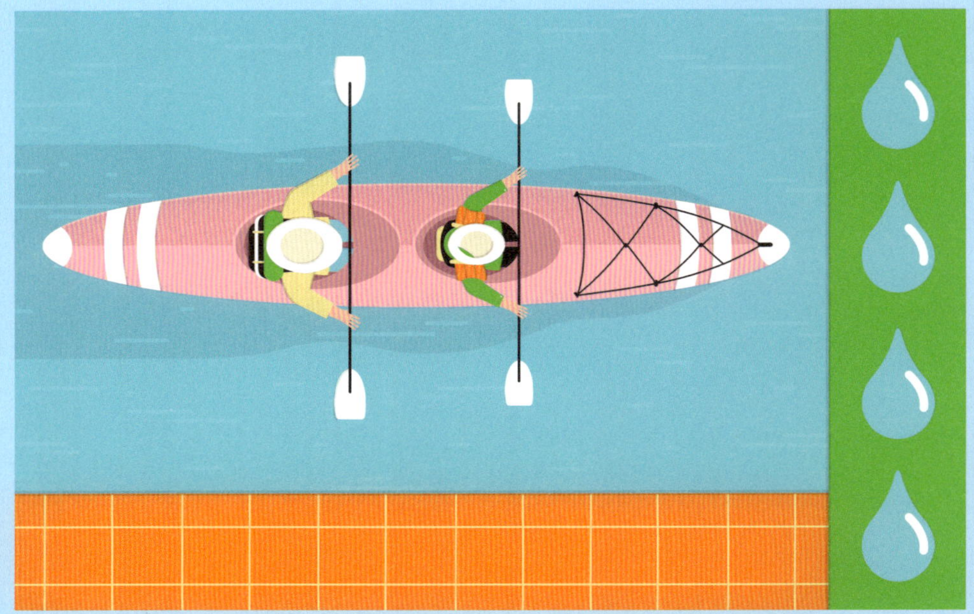

Middle schoolers strive for independence, to make their own maps of the world. It's an age when parents are often considered impediments to what would otherwise be a free and easy life, full of boundless possibilities. Since traveling necessarily requires a family to work as a unit, doing so with kids in this age range can be trying, to say the least. Not only will they want to go off on their own—something you will have to be vigilant about—but they may well be mortified by the very fact of your existence. But don't let that be a deterrent. Travel provides an opportunity to deepen a connection, or to reconnect, with a child that might be spending more and more time away from you.

Choosing a Destination

With this itinerant age group, a trip based in a single location means you won't have to set so many limits on your kids. If you're camping or posted up at a resort, there are far fewer options for roaming tweens than on a city trip, for example. Children will want to explore the surrounding areas, so choose a destination that has a suitably intriguing landscape—and one with kids' clubs, or activities such as swimming, hiking, kayaking, fishing, or foraging. From your base, plan day trips to sites in the wider region, and have your children participate in this process, as it will provide them with a sense of responsibility and increase their enjoyment.

How to Get There

For the modern family vacation, the road trip is a proven method of traveling from A to B, especially when it comes to the classic camping getaway. A roomy car or truck is a must, not only for the huge load of camping gear but also for the comfort of everyone on board. If you don't own or have easy access to a large vehicle, consider renting one or using a trailer. Pack your car, truck, or trailer the night before, and leave early the next day to maximize much-needed daylight for setting up camp at the other end—with kids around, this can take longer than you think. And make sure to bring a stock of snacks for the journey to avoid stopping too often along the way.

Checklist (For Camping)

- Reservations for campsite(s)
- Tent(s) (including poles and pegs)
- Canopy tent(s)
- Tarpaulins
- Sleeping bags and pillows and sleeping mats or air beds
- Clothing (including wet-weather gear) and footwear
- Swimwear and towels
- Foldable table and chairs
- Portable stove (with gas and matches or lighter)
- Frying pans and pots
- Cutting boards, knives, and cooking spoons
- Plates, bowls, cups, and mugs, water bottles, cutlery
- Cooler boxes (with freezable ice packs)
- Bucket to wash dishes, sponge, detergent, and dish towels
- Camping shower, soap, and shampoo
- Toothbrushes and toothpaste
- Sunscreen, insect repellent, and citronella candles
- First aid kit and medications
- Flashlights (with batteries)
- Trash bags
- Cameras
- Multiplayer games (such as beach tennis and volleyball)
- Bikes
- Equipment for outdoor activities (fishing, hiking, boogie boarding, etc.)

Where to Sleep

There are tents out there that sleep as many as 20 people. But given the proximity that camping entails, it's better to split things up. Parents can take up residence in a large two- or three-person tent, preferably with an awning and space for a makeshift kitchen. Then children of middle school age can sleep in their own two- or three-person tents, or share one with someone else. This will give them their own space to hang out in, or to retreat to after inevitable breakdowns of communication. (By the same token, if you're booking a hotel or resort, opt for a suite or two-bedroom unit.) Prepare sleeping spaces with air beds or mats, sleeping bags, pillows, and flashlights—and keep possessions away from the walls in case of rain.

Where to Eat

Whatever form your vacation takes, there's a strong likelihood your tweens won't want to stop what they're doing three times a day to sit in a dull restaurant with their parents. This headache can be easily avoided by packing healthy lunches and snacks: sandwiches, salads, nut bars, trail mix, and fresh fruit. If you're camping, planning out three meals per day is essential. Opt for something simple for breakfast, such as porridge or granola. For lunch, try to introduce some daily variation. Chickpea salads, hot dogs, grilled cheeses, and sandwiches are all preservable and delicious options.

Keep the limited cooking utensils and cleanup in mind when it comes to dinner. Try a few one-pot meals like nachos, pastas, and curries.

How to Move Around

Camping brings a range of options for exploring the immediate area. Hiking, for example, is a scenic way to navigate forests and coastal areas, offering stimulating opportunities for observing plants, birds, and other wildlife.

But do be careful to ensure your kids understand the importance of keeping to established trails. Biking is another fun way for middle schoolers to move around campsites and the areas surrounding them, especially if

the beach or lake is a long way from your tent. For trips further afield, to historical sites or natural phenomena, ask for your children's input.

Unexpected Twists

Children do get lost when exploring the great outdoors on hikes or even short jaunts through wooded areas, so it is imperative that they know what to do if this happens.

Make sure your kids are well-versed in these four key steps: First, they need to stay put as soon as they realize they've lost their bearings—tell them to hug a tree, make a nest, or something similar that conveys the point. Second, they need to call out for help, or at least make some repeated sound, every few minutes; a whistle reduces the energy a child can expend doing this. Third, they need to stay dry. Stuff a light poncho in their bag or pocket before setting out. Fourth, make sure they know help will be coming, whatever situation they find themselves in.

Hack

Allowing tweens to bring a friend on vacation is an absolute game changer in dealing with bad attitudes, and it's a strategy that could even result in an almost complete curtailment of difficult behavior.

A child with a friend around, with appearances to keep up and an identity to flesh out, is much less likely to act up. Additionally, if they have a companion, it's safer for them to go to nearby locations without you accompanying them.

For large families with children of different ages, bringing friends along also allows divergent age groups to split up and do different activities—and parents might even get the bonus of some quiet time without the kids around.

Rocky Mountain Refuge: A Spontaneous Escape to the Land of Amazement

YOHO NATIONAL PARK, CANADA

MARIA DEL ROSARIO, AIDAN (10), EMERY (7), AND EVE (3)

A free-spirited family finds respite from busy city life by taking a quick getaway to the majestic Canadian wilderness.

There are few travel experiences as adrenaline-filled and latent with potential as a spontaneous getaway: a jaunt to the countryside, a bolt to the old beach house, or a weekend road trip into the mountains. These escapes from the routine of everyday life have the power to refresh the senses and reignite the imagination of intrepid travelers looking for a quick burst of inspiration. What the short-notice escape lacks in preparation, it more than makes up for in epic memory-making potential. Like a slightly out of focus, candid photo that perfectly captures the magic of a specific moment, the snapshot of adventure an impulsive getaway provides is often priceless.

"Our best journeys are always the spontaneous ones," says lifestyle photographer Maria del Rosario, whose family prefers the excitement of last-minute getaways to trips organized months in advance. "We don't dwell too much on planning details; we just go for it. In our experience, that's how really special moments are made." Splitting her time between Vancouver and Calgary, two cities with views toward majestic mountain ranges, Maria is always eager to escape city life with her partner, Benjamin, and her children, Aidan, Emery, and Eve. All they need is a free weekend and favorable weather, and they'll pack and race to the car, ready to encounter the vast Canadian wilderness. "This particular

Yoho National Park was established in 1886, and ranges across 1,300 square kilometers (502 square miles) of rugged wilderness. Deer, moose, and grizzly bears roam the forest, crisscrossing valleys that are carpeted with wildflowers in summer and thick snows in winter.

During the long Canadian winter, visitor numbers dip, meaning fewer people, more quiet. Winter in Yoho is perfect for long, uninterrupted walks in the woods along the lakeshore, and the kids' first snowshoe journey over the surface of the frozen lake.

"When my kids were younger, I used to make them surprise backpacks before every trip that they weren't allowed to open until we were officially on the road."

trip was much the same—no planning, just a thought that arose and was executed right then and there," Maria says of the family's January 2018 getaway to Yoho National Park, a three-hour drive from their home in Calgary.

Long inhabited by the native Cree people, the park takes its name from their word yoho, meaning "amazement" or "awe"—and it's not hard to understand why that moniker was chosen. Yoho National Park, which was established as protected land in 1886, ranges across 1,300 square kilometers (502 square miles) of stunning, often rugged, wilderness teeming with wildlife. Deer, moose, and grizzly bears roam the forest, crisscrossing valleys that are carpeted with wildflowers in summer and thick snows in winter. The park also features an abundance of native tree species, including pine, spruce, and fir. Along with boasting some of the tallest mountains in the Canadian Rockies, Yoho is also home to Burgess Shale, an area of layered rock formations that have preserved unique fossils from the Cambrian period, and are more than 400 million years old.

During their spontaneous sojourn into Yoho, Maria and her family sequestered themselves at Emerald Lake Lodge, which overlooks a jade-colored ice field each winter. Built from hand-hewn timber and featuring centuries-old fireplaces, the lodge also includes an oak bar salvaged from a nineteenth-century Yukon saloon. According to Maria, a weekend at the lodge is a way to step back in time, to an era when modern cities were still a newfangled concept and nature was an ancient and ever-present adversary. "The log lodges have snow-covered roofs, glowing fireplaces, and no Wi-Fi," she says, hinting at the pleasure of time spent with her children, and without internet access. After all, it's increasingly uncommon today, when the web mediates much of our everyday reality, radically reducing opportunities to adventure out into the unknown. "These moments are more raw and wild," Maria says, "and there is a lot that can be learned trying to navigate them."

For Maria, the key is choosing the "wrong" time of year to venture into Yoho National Park. "Emerald Lake is spectacular in summer," she admits, "but it often draws big crowds that take away the feeling of solitude that comes from being out in the mountains." During the long Canadian winter, visitor numbers in the park dip, meaning fewer people, more quiet. Winter is perfect for long, uninterrupted walks in the woods along the lakeshore and the kids' first snowshoe journey over the surface of the frozen lake. Visiting Yoho off-season allowed the family to experience the park as a uniquely quiet refuge from their busy everyday lives back in the city. No crowds. No queues. No hustle and bustle. And, best of all, no distracting Wi-Fi for an entire weekend.

Maria and her children have set out on many "snapshot adventures" over the years. "When my kids were younger, I used to make them surprise backpacks before every trip that they weren't allowed to open until we were officially on the road," she recalls. It's a memory that Maria hopes her children will return to as they get older, along with fond recollections of time spent in Yoho. "With these trips, I hope to instill a lifelong appreciation of nature in my children," she says. Her family has discovered that building a lasting love for the outdoors doesn't mean embarking on extravagant, year-long voyages into the wilderness. Rather, Maria believes that regular day trips and impromptu weekend getaways can inspire her children to embrace both the wonders of the natural world and the power of the spontaneous adventure.

Explore More

YOHO NATIONAL PARK, EST. 1886

Yoho is located in British Columbia, on the western side of the Canadian Rockies. It was Canada's second national park after Banff (est. 1885). Today the park is part of a UNESCO World Heritage Site.

ROCKY MOUNTAIN HIGH

Yoho is a big, wild place. Spanning more than 1,300 square kilometers (502 square miles), the park features 61 lakes and ponds within its boundaries (Emerald Lake is the largest), and 28 mountain peaks higher than 3,000 meters (9,843 feet).

ADVENTURE TIME

Yoho provides opportunities for camping, fishing, mountain climbing, cross country skiing, snowshoeing, exploring waterfalls, and hiking the park's more than 400 kilometers (249 miles) of designated trails.

WATCH FOR WILDLIFE

The park is home to a menagerie of creatures, including: squirrels, chipmunks, badgers, lynx, cougars, wolverines, marmots, mountain goats, elk, moose, as well as black and grizzly bears.

WHAT THE SHALE?

Discovered by paleontologist Charles Walcott in 1909, Burgess Shale has been the site of extensive study and excavations by scientists from around the world. It was designated as a UNESCO World Heritage Site in 1980.

The Road Less Traveled: Nomadic Living in a Hostel on Wheels

ACROSS EUROPE

VAL COOK AND TIM BOFFE, FENNA (5), ZIGGY (1), AND LEWIS THE DOG

An enterprising family converts a bus into a hostel, the road into their home, and the world into a classroom.

A man walks into a bar in the alpine village of Risoul, France. He orders a beer. His name is Tim. The bartender that evening is Valerie, a self-described nomad who has been crisscrossing the globe since she graduated from high school. After years of bouncing between the surf towns of Europe and Australia and the ski towns of Canada and Switzerland, Val is trying to decide what to do, or—perhaps more importantly—where to go next. University was an option. Then again, she had always dreamed of running a hostel someday. Tim and Val start to chat. That was 2011. "It was that evening in Risoul," recalls Val, "that our adventure began."

A year later, Val and Tim were traveling the world together, on a budget of €9 ($10) per day per person, plus €2 ($2) a day for their dog Lewis. While exploring Central America, they had an "epiphany" that would change the course of their future by allowing them to combine their passions for travel, ski and snowboard instructing, hiking, cooking, photography, and meeting new people. "We had talked about the idea of converting an American school bus into a mobile home," Val says, "but now we started to think we could make a business out of the concept by creating a 'hostel on wheels' that would allow us—and our guests—to chase the snow from one ski resort to another."

THE NOMADS BUS
1-TKU-047

“We had an amazing first summer,” says Valerie Cook, “getting to know the ins and outs of the bus itself, but also how to manage the guests, the website, bookings, parking, maintenance—all while we had a one-year-old with us.”

"Norway stole our hearts, so we spent two winter seasons and three summers there, mostly above the arctic circle. The bus just belonged there; there was no place else we wanted to be."

"Living on the bus enabled us to spend most of our time in the mountains and with our kids. It was a kind of school for all of us, but especially the kids, who got their first exposure to adventure—to skiing, hiking, meeting new people, and playing outside."

“We had talked about the idea of converting an American school bus into a mobile home,” says Valerie Cook, “but now we started to think we could make a business out of the concept by creating a ‘hostel on wheels.’”

PICT
URE

"We want to inspire people to get outside and have an adventure. We really believe it's possible for people to do what they love to do. This is the message we want to share through all our projects, and the lesson we want to share with our kids."

“For us, ‘adventure parenting’ means letting our kids learn by doing. We let them go barefoot as much as possible, climb steep cliffs, or sometimes go without a jacket if they’re being stubborn.”

After a successful crowdfunding campaign raised more than €23,000 ($25,500), the couple was able to purchase a decommissioned American school bus on eBay and have it shipped from Florida to Belgium. “It took us more than a year and a half to get the bus road-ready,” Val recalls, “and in the meantime we also had a baby. But we’ve never run away from a challenge; that’s just the way we are.” The renovated bus featured a master bedroom, a lounge, six bunk beds for guests, a kitchen, a compost toilet, a sun deck on the roof, and lots of storage to haul bouldering, fishing, ski, surf, and skate gear. Finally, in May 2016, Val, Tim, and their little daughter Fenna climbed aboard the Nomads Bus, Europe’s first “hostel on wheels” and made their way south, toward the surf towns of the Mediterranean coast.

“We had an amazing first summer,” Val says, “getting to know the ins and outs of the bus itself, but also how to manage the guests, the website, bookings, parking, maintenance—all while we had a one-year-old with us.” That first year, the family lived on the bus, which, Val says, “actually felt huge when we didn’t have guests.” But contrary to the assumptions of many people, life wasn’t an endless roving vacation. “Actually it was the opposite: cooking, driving, planning, cleaning, entertaining, running all the social media, and doing so much more, all day, every day,” says Val. “Yes, it’s a fun, amazing lifestyle, but it was also insanely hard work.”

The Nomads Bus could host up to six guests at a time plus Val, Tim, and Fenna in their private quarters, and no two journeys were ever the same. For three years, the family hosted guests from all over the world as they toured Europe guiding hiking, surf, ski, and snowboard trips. Of all the places they visited, Norway was by far their favorite destination. “Norway stole our hearts,” Val says, “so we spent two winter seasons and three summers there, mostly above the arctic circle. The bus just belonged there; there was no place else we wanted to be.”

In the spring of 2019, Val and Tim’s second child Ziggy was born. The family moved into a camper van that traveled alongside the bus, and spent the next year on the road, welcoming guests and guiding trips through Norway. In the spring of 2020, they decided it was time to move on to a new adventure, and so they handed over the keys to another couple who will continue to operate the hostel on wheels after some much-needed renovations are completed.

Looking back, Val and Tim deeply cherish the unique experience of the Nomads Bus. “I loved sharing this journey with the kids,” Val says, “and I can still see the smiles on their faces when we’d wake up in a new place every morning. Living on the bus enabled us to spend most of our time in the mountains and with our kids. It was a kind of school for all of us, but especially the kids who got their first exposure to adventure—to skiing, hiking, meeting new people, and playing outside.”

Today, Val and Tim have a new dream for the future: to create a Nomads Lodge somewhere off the beaten path, where they can host guests looking to escape modern city life and reconnect with nature. In the meantime, the couple has launched “Nomads Vibes,” a curated outdoor adventure guide where they share travel tips and lessons learned from their many years of exploring Europe.

“In everything we do, we want to inspire people to get outside and have an adventure,” Val says. “We really believe it’s possible for people to do what they love to do. We try to live every day with integrity, and do what feels right. This is the message we want to share through all our projects and, most of all, it’s the lesson we want to share with our kids.”

Explore More

THE EUROPEAN ROAD TRIP
With its open borders and a wealth of distinct cultures, diverse landscapes, and historic cities and sites located relatively very close together, Europe is an ideal place for a family road trip.

CHECK YOUR CHECKLIST
Before you hit the road, make sure you have the right type of driver’s license, insurance, passport or visa, and credit card (rental agencies are particular about this one). Plus, you’re gonna need lots of snacks.

SAFETY FIRST
Whether you’re hiring, buying, or borrowing a car for your trip, make sure to familiarize yourself with the local traffic laws in each country you plan to visit (they can differ slightly).

STOP AND SMELL THE ROSES
You can break up the longer drives with regular stops in alpine towns, at roadside Polish barbecue stands, or in picturesque French villages. Besides, mom and dad are going to “need” plenty of coffee breaks.

“BUCKET LIST” EU ROAD TRIPS
Romantic Road (Germany), Route One (Iceland), Ring of Kerry (Ireland), North Coast 500 (Scotland), Porto to Algarve (Portugal), the Amalfi Coast (Italy), Vienna to Geneva (Austria and Switzerland).

The Meeting of Waters: A Young Explorer's Journey into Amazonia

MANAUS AND THE RIO NEGRO, BRAZIL

KARILYN OWEN AND CIAN BYRNE (9)

A mother-son team of adventurers discovers flora, fauna, and friendship on a journey down the Amazon's Rio Negro.

An adventurous life can begin at any age. In fact, Sir Edmund Hillary made his first major ascent when he was only 20, the American aviator Elinor Smith already had her pilot's licence at 16, and survivalist Bear Grylls first learned to climb and sail as a little boy. For nine-year-old Cian Byrne, his craving for exploration and excitement began almost from the moment he was born.

"He went to seven countries in the first year of his life," says Karilyn Owen, Cian's mom and regular travel partner. The eager young adventurer has not looked back since, and his encounters with diverse environments and cultures have come to profoundly shape his ideas about the world and his future. Having lived the first two years of his life in India, today he and his mother are based in the United States. Together, they frequently venture to lands near and far, from their home country's national parks to as far afield as South Africa and Sweden, Cambodia and the Cook Islands. "He has a deep love and knowledge of nature and science that I can't even comprehend," Karilyn says. Is it any wonder that Cian now dreams of becoming a wildlife photographer for *National Geographic?*

So Cian was overjoyed when, in 2018, his mother dreamed up an irresistible adventure: visiting the Rio Negro ("Black River"), a lively tributary of the Amazon River in Brazil. In its snaking, seemingly endless waterways, the Rio Negro sustains around 700 known

The Rio Negro is a lively tributary of the Amazon River in Brazil. In its snaking, seemingly endless waterways, the Rio Negro sustains around 700 known species of fish, with many more undocumented specimens hidden beneath the dark waters.

From their base in the U.S., Karilyn and her son frequently venture to lands as far afield as South Africa and Sweden, Cambodia and the Cook Islands. "Cian has a deep love and knowledge of nature and science that I can't even comprehend," Karilyn says.

Seeing the Meeting of Rivers with his own eyes, and trying to grasp the vast diversity of the flora and fauna—these are memories that have embedded themselves in Cian's mind forever, and further ignited his dreams of becoming a wildlife photographer.

"For Cian, our time on the Amazon River was all about experiencing one of the world's most amazing ecosystems up close. I know these epic experiences will linger within him, and help guide him through the world."

species of fish, with many more undocumented specimens hidden beneath the dark waters—a mysterious fact that would have any young explorer gazing into the depths for hours on end. And, once his journey began, that's exactly how Cian spent much of his time.

For the first part of their eight-day trip, run by eco-minded organization Our Whole Village, Karilyn and Cian spent two days in the city of Manaus. From here, the pair was ferried on a local boat to view the "Meeting of Waters," an impressive natural phenomenon where the dark-colored Rio Negro and the paler Amazon River meet but don't immediately blend together. "Think of one as melted milk chocolate, and the other as coffee," Cian explained to his mother. "As they meet, they can't mix until their consistency and temperature become one." Later that day, Cian offered Karilyn more helpful information during a visit to a local village. As a bowl of fried ants was passed between locals and members of the tour group, Cian, who had already indulged, encouraged his hesitant mother: "They taste like kale chips," he assured her. Karilyn begs to differ. "I will state for the record they did not taste like my homemade kale chips at all!"

The mother-and-son duo then embarked on their most anticipated leg of the journey: four days navigating the Rio Negro on a beautiful three-tiered wooden boat named *Jacaré Açu*. "It was a family-focused tour, so all the guests had kids, and, luckily for us parents, they got along beautifully," Karilyn says. And since there was no Wi-Fi on the boat, she was delighted at the opportunity to socialize with the harmonious group. After long days spent hiking in the rain forest, fishing for piranhas, and scanning the dark waters for pink river dolphins and caimans, "none of us retreated to our cabins," Karilyn recalls. "Instead, we hung out on the deck and listened to the kids sing the songs they had practiced all day. The sense of comradery we felt is difficult to put in words."

Part of that comradery might have come from an idea of responsible tourism shared among the tour members. Toward the end of the journey, they stopped to visit a small village on the Rio Negro. Such situations initially felt rather "delicate," given their potential to be invasive and even exploitative. But, with the children around, the parents' reservations were quickly eased. "During that visit, a rainstorm drenched the village, making us all rush inside a tiny schoolhouse to seek shelter," Karilyn says. "The local kids took this as an opportunity to play, and Cian couldn't resist the temptation to join in building a mud river to race leaf boats, leaving differences of language and culture behind."

"For Cian, our time on the Amazon was all about experiencing one of the world's most amazing ecosystems up close," Karilyn says. Seeing the Meeting of Rivers with his own eyes, trying to grasp the vast diversity of flora and fauna, and capturing glimpses of the Amazon's rare pink river dolphin—these are memories that have embedded themselves in the boy's mind forever, and further ignited his dreams of becoming a wildlife photographer. "I know these epic experiences will linger within him, and help guide him through the world," says Karilyn.

But like all true adventurers, Cian isn't even close to being finished exploring Earth's bio and cultural diversity. Next up on the young man's "must-see" travel destinations: Madagascar and Antarctica. Now he just needs to convince his mom.

Explore More

THE LAST GREAT RAIN FOREST
Although it is one of the most bio-diverse areas on the planet, the Amazon rain forest is also a troubled region, which means it is more important than ever to choose ethical travel in this unique region.

A REGION IN CRISIS
The biggest threat to the rain forest continues to be deforestation. By raising awareness and encouraging engagement, responsible ecotourism can support a multi-tiered approach to protecting this vital region.

EXPERIENCE AMAZONIA
The Amazon rain forest covers more than five million square kilometers (1.9 million square miles) spread over nine countries (60 percent in Brazil). Each nation has ways to visit responsibly; from volunteer tours to wildlife rescue and plant medicine programs.

FIND A TOUR THAT GIVES BACK
By directly donating to projects in family health, education, and conservation, Our Whole Village is a good example of a tour company that supports the communities where it operates its adventures.

YOU NEED A QUALIFIED GUIDE
Not only will a professional guide know how to safely navigate forests and waterways, they will also know the area's flora and fauna, and will have relationships with local communities and indigenous groups.

Living the Dream: A Once-in-a-Lifetime Safari Adventure

KENYA, TANZANIA, AND ZANZIBAR

JAIMEE GONG AND CYRIL MEGRET, GENJI (PRE-TEEN), LILYMIEL (TEENAGER), AND GRANDMA JANICE

Three generations come together for an epic family adventure: an 11-day "flying safari" through Kenya and Tanzania.

The African safari is an unparalleled travel experience: a surreal blend of rugged adventure, otherworldly landscapes, and up-close encounters with some of the world's most fascinating wildlife. For most of us, the safari will forever remain the stuff of picture books and nature documentaries. But for those able to make the journey, it can be a sublime and life-changing milestone.

For Jaimee Gong and her family, stepping into the African savannah felt like entering a dream. "In an instant, there were zebras, elephants, giraffes, and all kinds of birds right there in front of us," she says. "The whole scene was like something a child had painted from their imagination; it didn't feel real, but it was." Jaimee embarked on the epic trip with her husband Cyril Megret, their two children, Genji and Lilymiel, and her mother Janice—three generations gathered together for one ambitious, unforgettable vacation. Surprisingly, it wasn't the zoo-inspired fantasies of Jaimee's kids that brought the family all the way from France to Africa, but grandma Janice's "bucket list" wish. "I remembered how quickly my own children had reached their older adolescent years and then shown less interest in family outings," says Janice. "So the time was right for a multi-generational trek together." In late July 2018, the family began an 11-day excursion with a "flying safari." Using small aircraft or helicopters to fly between

ANGAMA
MARA

The “flying safari” allowed the family to travel between locations via small aircraft and, thus, they could take in immense expanses of flora and fauna from above, and also reach remote, isolated areas where wildlife might be more abundant.

The African safari is an unparalleled travel experience: a surreal blend of rugged adventure, otherworldly landscapes, and up-close encounters with some of the world's most fascinating wildlife.

At journey's end, the excitement of the family's safari adventure was rounded out with a beach vacation on the island of Zanzibar, off the coast of Tanzania, shortly before the family returned home to France.

"In an instant, there were zebras, elephants, giraffes, and all kinds of birds right there in front of us. The whole scene was like something a child had painted from their imagination; it didn't feel real, but it was."

locations, they could take in immense expanses of flora and fauna from above, and also reach remote, isolated areas where wildlife might be more abundant. Together they soared over deserts and grasslands, before being picked up by knowledgeable camp staff in 4×4s and taken to their lodgings, which usually held no more than 10 tents per site. "The interiors of the tents were probably more charming than many hotels," Jaimee recalls.

Beginning their adventure in Nairobi, Kenya, the crew journeyed to the luxurious campsites of Lewa Safari Camp, just north of Mount Kenya, and Angama Mara, overlooking the renowned savannah of Maasai Mara. Jaimee was particularly impressed by the Angama Mara accommodations, where, she says, "we had an exceptional guide who was able to observe wildlife patterns and movements in order to find the animals better." Crossing from Kenya into Tanzania, the family chanced upon a truly majestic scene: near the border, on the Mara River, they witnessed the drama of an animal river crossing. "Herds of wildebeests ran and swam across the river," Jaimee says, "with hippos, zebras, and hungry crocodiles in the mix—a truly unique experience that goes beyond words."

Janice quickly picked up on the reason they were able to have such close encounters with wildlife: "The animals don't recognize the 4×4 vehicles as either threat or prey," she says. For Janice, the thrill of watching the natural theatrics on display was heightened by watching her grandchildren's pleasure. "Riding along in the vehicles, the children were agile and quick to snap photos of animals with their mouths open, or spot them behind bushes and in trees eating their prey," she says.

Moving southeast from the Mara River, the family entered the Serengeti—Maasai for "endless plains"—a protected area of 30,000 square kilometers (11,583 square miles). On the southern edge of the grasslands, they stayed at Ubuntu Migration Camp, known for its staff's honed tracking of wildebeests. From there, they ventured east to Lemala Ngorongoro Camp, which sits inside the World Heritage Site of the Ngorongoro Conservation Area. Here they visited the famous crater that shares its name with the reserve—the largest inactive and unfilled caldera in the world. In the midst of these expeditions, tsetse flies, capable of delivering nasty bites, were a constant annoyance. "They loved my son!" Jaimee exclaims. It was some time before the family realized that the blue-and-black flags they were seeing everywhere were in fact tsetse fly traps, and that Genji's beloved blue-and-black sweater was acting as a beacon for the pesky insects—"Oops," Jaimee says. "He covered up his sweatshirt, and it was a miracle. No more flies!"

At journey's end, the excitement of the safari trip was rounded out with a beach vacation on the island of Zanzibar, off the coast of Tanzania, shortly before the family returned home to France. For Janice, the safari was a once-in-a-lifetime experience, made even more special by the eager participation of her grandchildren. "An outward sense of wonderment and curiosity prevails with the presence of young kids," she says. "Lilymiel and Genji were so amped up; they couldn't stop talking about their favorite parts of the trip," Jaimee adds. "I made a photo album to keep as a souvenir. Looking at it helps them remember the amazing experience. They look at it all the time and discuss it over and over again." It appears that what began as an adventure that seemingly "couldn't be real" exists now as memories that can always be returned to—pages in a book all the family's own.

Explore More

ETHICAL AFRICAN SAFARIS
The safari industry has a complex (often sad) past and a delicate present. It's up to you to choose an ethical option that actually helps to support (not hurt) local communities and that promotes wildlife conservation.

ASK THE RIGHT QUESTIONS
Do all your research and remember to think bigger than price. The way safari companies manage guests, staff, and wildlife truly matters. Sites like responsibletravel.com can help you find ethical tour options.

FOLLOW THE LEADER
Safari guides know what they are talking about. Usually, they are locals with a lifetime of knowledge about the land, the animals, and the real dangers at hand in the bush. Take their advice seriously.

RESPECT. RESPECT. RESPECT
You may go on a safari for the animals, but don't forget the local people, landscapes, economies, and communities that your trip will impact. Focus on being respectful and, when in doubt, ask a guide for help.

THE JOURNEY STARTS NOW
Look to sites like responsibletravel.com to find ethical options like: Great Plains Conservation (Botswana), Scenic Air Safaris (Kenya), Bisate Lodge (Rwanda), and Rhino Conservation Safari (S. Africa).

TRAVEL TIPS: THIRTEEN AND UP

Teenagers need encouragement and room to breathe. What they don't need is a shadowy parental presence intent on setting limits—the age for that is over. As a parent of a teen, you no longer exclusively govern their world, and there is no reason why children with budding intellects should fall into line with your preferences and opinions. Instead, look at teenagers as individuals with their own likes and dislikes, whatever those may be. Rather than setting limits and creating tensions that can undermine the enjoyment of a trip, try to let things go—unless, of course, they have really stepped out of line. Giving teenagers space to assert themselves can be the key to a successful vacation.

Choosing a Destination

Involve teenagers in the early planning stages of a trip. Find out where they would like to go and what they would like to do and see. This is especially important if you have more than one child, as interests could differ considerably.

If that's the case, think about splitting a holiday into sections that line up with the interests of each family member. In general, look for destinations that provide opportunities for teens to push (and prove) themselves, through activities such as skiing, snorkeling, and trekking.

Experiences like these give them bragging rights and help them develop confidence. Now that your kids are more independent, you can broaden your horizons and visit distant countries that might otherwise have been difficult to navigate.

How to Get There

Entertainment matters when traveling with teens. If you're going further afield via long-haul flights, fly with an airline that has a well-reviewed catalog of movies and series. Emirates, Qatar Airways, Singapore Airlines, Virgin Atlantic, and Delta Air Lines are all companies that offer a high standard of entertainment.

Just remember to bring your own headsets—provided devices are notoriously lo-fi. And now that free in-flight Wi-Fi has become a possibility, see if you can book with an airline that provides this modern luxury. If that's not possible, suggest your teenager downloads podcasts and videos from YouTube before the flight takes off, or, for that matter, before you embark on any form of travel.

Checklist (For Distant Destinations)

- Travel documents (passports, visas, insurance, reservation information)
- Clothes (a week's worth, as access to washing facilities could be intermittent)
- One evening outfit
- Extra socks and underwear
- Footwear (open and closed)
- Swimwear (two options)
- Light towels (such as those made of microfiber)
- Sunglasses
- Hats
- Snacks
- Magazines (for flight)
- Headphones
- Earplugs
- Lip balm
- Toothbrushes and toothpaste
- Soap and shampoo
- Hairbrush or comb
- Face cleanser (and other skincare)
- Deodorant
- High SPF sunscreen
- Insect repellent
- First aid kit and medications
- Electronic devices (smartphones, tablets, laptops)
- Books about destination
- Notebooks for journal entries
- A deck of cards (for locations without internet)

Where to Sleep

The first thing to consider when booking a hotel or private home is location. Being near to a city center with roaming options for restless teenagers will help to alleviate cabin fever—a benefit that may outweigh the extra cost.

Keep in mind that teens will want to shut themselves away, and sleep in. Be lenient on them—it means one less battle to fight while traveling. In a family with more than one teenager, sharing a large room is likely a better solution than booking a separate one for them, as you can at least be sure they will get some sleep. If hotels are not in your price range—many begin charging adult rates for teens—staying in hostels is a good way to make things cheaper.

Where to Eat

At this age, kids have a light-speed metabolism. Make sure you carry a stock of energy-delivering supplies to combat the grumpiness associated with hunger—think granola bars, fresh fruit, and the odd sweet treat. When choosing a restaurant, let teenagers have their pick some of the time, even if that means eating burgers and fries more than you would like. If kids aren't interested in food, try bringing them along to cooking classes, which are sometimes organized through hotels and hostels, or can be found online.

Not only will this introduce teens to the beauty of local cuisines, but it might also ignite a real interest in food—and make a pleasurable stroll down street-food alleys that much more feasible.

How to Move Around

Navigating urban areas alone is a possibility for teenagers. Whether this should be encouraged depends on the general safety of your location, and on the age and maturity level of your kids. If you're uncomfortable with them traveling alone on public transport, consider substituting that for

a walk around the block, or to a nearby destination. If that's still not an option, suggest you all go on a walking tour.

Guided by knowledgeable residents who will inform you about historical sites, they are a great way to learn about the city you are visiting. When you're traveling as a large family unit, especially going to and from the airport, keep in mind that a taxi is often more economical than buying individual tickets for public transport.

Unexpected Twists

Teenage temper tantrums should be handled sensitively on vacation. When things go wrong, there are fewer places for them to retreat to, and they are also without the familiar comforts of home that would usually assist in settling things down.

If you do face a teenage meltdown, remember to keep yourself under control, no matter how flagrant their behavior. An angry teen does not need further excuses to lash out.

Make a specific time to talk when the mood has calmed and be very clear on the types of behavior you deem unacceptable—and cut off all communication when such acts occur. Lastly, remind yourself to be patient with your teen. Their behavior can change, but it will take time.

Hacks

No one wants to take a teenager on vacation only to watch them gaze into the infinite abyss of their smartphone whenever there's a free moment. But neither do you want to create a point of constant contention by insisting they do not use them.

One way around this is to set up phone-free times during dinnertime, or for an hour or two on a road trip. This strategy, as long as it's laid out clearly ahead of time, can take a lot of the tension out of policing this problem. Of course, you could take a vacation, or part of it, in a location that does not have internet access, like a remote resort or coastal area.

It's Always Summer at Wandawega: A Historic American Getaway Lives On

Camp Wandawega is a quirky, no-frills resort that was once home to a speakeasy, a secret hideout for Chicago mobsters, and a brothel. Today, it offers families the opportunity to experience the simple pleasures of a simpler time.

DAVID HERNANDEZ AND TEREASA SURRATT, CHARLIE (10)

"When we were kids, my friends and I would sit around the campfire and fantasize about someday having our own cabins here by the lake. Back then, it never occurred to me that I might actually own the whole summer camp—let alone raise my family here." And yet, more than three decades later, David Hernandez and his wife Tereasa Surratt do own the camp he visited each summer as a boy.

Known today as Camp Wandawega, this iconic American summer camp has a stranger-than-fiction history that stretches back to the 1920s and is as fantastic as any tall tale told "round a campfire;" before it was a summer camp, the property had been home to a speakeasy, a secret hideout for Chicago mobsters, and a brothel. But the Camp Wandawega of today also has an ambitious and uniquely modern mission: to both preserve the historic soul of the place and be the kind of inclusive, open-hearted destination where guests can come to enjoy the quiet, leafy woods of Walworth County, Wisconsin, for "a refreshing respite from 'the real world.'"

For David, camp was the scene of some of his happiest childhood memories: climbing trees, swimming in the lake, and generally making mischief. So, when the property came up for sale in 2004, he couldn't bear to see it sold off to someone

"When we were kids, my friends and I would sit around the campfire and fantasize about someday having our own cabins here by the lake. Back then, it never occurred to me that I might actually own the whole summer camp."

“Tom’s Treehouse” is a relatively new addition to Camp Wandawega. Three stories tall and anchored to a sturdy elm tree, this architectural highlight was built entirely by volunteers as a memorial for co-owner Tereasa Surratt’s father.

"We'd like to think this strange and wonderful place will be here forever, and we're just the latest cast of characters put in charge. And if we're not adding a little crazy here and there, well then we're not very good camp counselors, are we?"

who might subdivide it and erase more than 75 years of history. "I would have been heartbroken if someone else got it," he recalls. And so, he and Tereasa decided to save the sacred old place. "It had so much history and so much potential," Tereasa recalls. "I couldn't help wondering how many lost stories were waiting to be discovered around the property, and how many more were just waiting to be written."

When David and Tereasa took over, the property and all of its buildings were in bad shape. After years of neglect, there were broken windows, mold and mildew growing everywhere, and rooms overflowing with decades' worth of long-forgotten junk. The historic Bunkhouse, Lakeside Cabin, and Lodge—along with the boat dock, sandy beach, and tennis court—were in a state of near-total disrepair. So, armed with a big, ambitious vision, lots of optimism, and a cadre of good friends willing to work for free, David and Tereasa got to work.

In time, the property began to emerge from its disheveled state. Resurrected and minimally-modernized, it now features several original buildings alongside an eclectic collection of new structures, including "Tom's Treehouse," the architectural highlight of the camp. Three stories high and anchored to an elm tree, the treehouse was built entirely by volunteers as a memorial for Tereasa's father. Today, Wandawega is both a time capsule and a time machine, ready to transport guests to a simpler era and help them achieve a more peaceful state of mind. Like a vintage toy village come to life, it exists to be explored and enjoyed by kids of all ages.

Since the day David and Tereasa reopened the property to guests, old friends and new have been coming here to get away for a few days, to rediscover camp life with their kids, and ease into the cool embrace of Lake Wandawega. When asked what people love most about coming to stay, David explains, "It sounds like a cliché when I talk about 'the simple pleasures of a simpler time' but it's true. Families can be families here, devoid of the trappings of modern life—no televisions, no internet, no distractions. So, they sit around a campfire, pile into rowboats, and take walks in the woods. Youngsters embrace the activities with a sense of wonder, grown-ups embrace them with childlike delight and nostalgia. Whether it's fishing, swimming, shuffleboard, exploring a treehouse, working on traditional camp crafts—these activities put people of all ages on the same level, and there's something magical about that."

“Whether it’s fishing, swimming, shuffleboard, exploring a tree-house, working on traditional camp crafts—these activities put people of all ages on the same level, and there’s something magical about that.”

"Families can be families here, devoid of the trappings of modern life—no internet, no distractions," says David Hernandez. "Youngsters embrace the activities with a sense of wonder, grown-ups embrace them with a childlike delight and nostalgia."

"None of us are really able to acknowledge that 'the good old days' are happening right now. We get so caught up in what's next. But, sooner than we think, we'll be looking back at this time and wishing we had it back."

Each summer, the family shares Camp Wandawega with non-profit organizations who put on camps for kids, young artists, musicians, and local church groups, endeavors that Tereasa Surratt calls "the most emotionally fulfilling money-losers ever."

Since 2004, David Hernandez and Tereasa Surratt have been the co-owners and caretakers of Camp Wandawega, the summer camp David attended throughout his childhood. Their daughter Charlie was born in 2010.

"I get choked up every time I see my daughter playing in the lake with my mom and dad, just like I did nearly 50 years before her. For all that's changed in the world, these simple pleasures of a simpler time have remained exactly the same."

For the couple, one of the most gratifying aspects of the ongoing project of restoration, has been sharing this unique piece of Americana with others. "We get to meet folks from all over who are getting away from the pressures of everyday life," David says, "and we get caught up in that same positive energy; we get to see these people at their best—when they're reconnecting with each other and with nature, making new friends, and just plain letting their guard down." Each summer, the couple shares the property with non-profit organizations who put on camps for kids, young artists, musicians, and local church groups, endeavors Tereasa calls "the most emotionally fulfilling money-losers ever."

Wandawega has also become a second home for the family, who split their time between camp and their home in Chicago. Their daughter Charlie, who was born in 2010, has, quite literally, grown up at camp. "It's very much a 'country mouse, city mouse' experience for Charlie," Tereasa says. "In Chicago, our lives are driven by a schedule, with little room for spontaneity. When we're at Camp Wandawega, our family is able to shift gears entirely. It's definitely a second full-time job, but after a stressful week working in the corporate world, camp is the perfect remedy: we get to come here and dig a trench, clear some trees, or host an event—the kind of stuff that provides all three of us with balance and perspective."

For David and Tereasa, Camp Wandawega has been more than just a passion project: it is an opportunity for them to build new relationships: "People come from all walks of life, all belief systems, all persuasions," Tereasa says. "Charlie really gets to know many of these people: to welcome them, give them tours, and practice her own version of gracious hospitality." For David, the fact that Wandawega is Charlie's second home is only fitting. "It means a lot to see her grow up here; I get choked up every time I walk to the hillside overlooking the beach and see her playing in the lake with my mom and dad, just like I did nearly 50 years before her. For all that's changed in the world, these simple pleasures of a simpler time have remained exactly the same."

“The Tipi” is a modern canvas recreation of classic Native American designs and is nestled in a hidden clearing overlooking the lake.

This Land is Our Land: A Tour of America's National Parks

NATIONAL PARKS, USA

DAVID AND MADISON BOWMAN, GRAHAM (3) AND MARGARET (1)

To experience the best of America, the Bowman family embarked on a quest to visit each of the country's national parks.

David and Madison Bowman have always had a thing for road trips. "One of the first plans we made after we met was to form a band and tour random truck stops across the country," David says. "We called it *The Great American Truck Stop Tour.* We wanted to play music, but mostly we wanted to see America through the everyday places where people's lives play out." The band never made it out on the road ("we barely made it out of our living room," Madison jokes), but the dream of traveling the country never went away.

In the years before their kids were born, the couple lived briefly in San Francisco and Utah, before settling in New York City and welcoming two kids, Graham and Margaret. "David had a great job as a graphic designer, and I was a full-time mom trying to do some writing on the side," Madison says. "But we still had a lot of goals; we didn't want to save for retirement or squeeze into two weeks of vacation per year." For David, early signs of burnout were appearing. "We were at a point where we were evaluating

The Bowmans hit the road in April 2017, with the goal of touring all 59 of America's national parks (there are now 62). To do this, they came up with a zig-zagging route that would allow them to "follow the weather" as they looped across the country.

As for parenting on the road, "it looked a lot like parenting in any other situation," David Bowman says. "Nap times were still a struggle, bedtime was still a struggle, but we tried to hang on to some semblance of routine, and somehow it worked."

what we wanted out of our lives and jobs," he says, "and I knew I wanted to make a fundamental change."

So, the couple put pen to paper and outlined their ideal American road trip. At the top of that list was: (1) to live in a bus and (2) to visit all of America's national parks. Embarking on an "American Field Trip" would fulfill a lifelong dream, while also providing firsthand knowledge of the complex issues facing public land preservation in North America. Though the timing for a trip like this would never be perfect, "we weren't getting any younger and we knew if we didn't do it now, the chance might just pass us by," says David. "So we started figuring out what we needed to keep everybody happy and how we could make enough money to keep gas in the tank."

They bought a secondhand Ford shuttle bus—which they stripped and completely retooled—and hit the road in April 2017, with the goal of touring all 59 of America's national parks (there are now 62). To do this, they came up with a zig-zagging route that would allow them to "follow the weather" as they looped across the country. From New York, they traveled through the midwestern states, the Pacific Northwest, and into Alaska, where they spent the summer before heading back through the midwest, down

"National parks in America are a meeting place for people from different cultures and backgrounds to come together and share this amazing natural space—to have fun and learn and be challenged. That's something we believe is vital to preserve."

The Bryce Canyon National Park was number 51 of the Bowman's list. It is located in southwestern Utah and provides spectacular views with its red, orange, and white colors of the rocks.

“The outdoors became such a cathartic force for our family,” David says. “We learned that when our kids are put in challenging situations, they have more fun than when they’re in environments that don’t present them with anything new.”

The United States has 62 protected areas, knows as national parks. The National Park Service, founded in 1916, was created to conserve the scenery, the natural and historic objects, and wildlife therein.

"You get to a point in life when you think, 'is *this* what we dreamed about doing when we grew up?' We couldn't help but wonder if it was still possible to do some of those crazy things we dreamed about as kids."

into Florida and eventually meandering back to the West Coast, completing their journey in Alaska in October 2018. Although each park was fascinating in its own way, Alaska was a highlight: "Katmai National Park was a peak life experience for us," Madison says. "It's the most beautiful place in the world."

The family spent about a week in each park, getting to know people and the unique environmental issues facing the land. "In the last decade, visitorship has skyrocketed," David explains. "This combined with the fact that the current government is defunding public lands and trying to deregulate its usage, is creating this immense and complex conflict. National parks in America are a meeting place for people from different cultures and backgrounds to come together and share this amazing natural space—to have fun and learn and be challenged. That's something we believe is vital to preserve."

As for parenting on the road, it looked a lot like parenting in any other situation. "Nap times were still a struggle, bedtime was still a struggle, but we tried to hang on to some semblance of routine, and somehow it worked," David explains. "Converting the bus into a home meant our kids could sleep in the same beds every night. It gave them a sense of security and consistency no matter where we traveled. Still," David says, "it's never as glamorous as it looks online. Taking care of kids while traveling is always difficult; you've just gotta take it one day at a time, stay flexible, and keep expectations low, so you're able to respond to changes in the weather or things that happen in the moment."

The pair admits there were many times when they felt like "cashing in and going home." But, then, the family would spend a day hiking or exploring together, and find the will to press on. "The outdoors became such a cathartic force for our family," David says. "We learned that when our kids are put in challenging situations, they have more fun than when they're in environments that don't present them with anything new." The couple hopes that their family's big adventure will encourage their kids to go out and try things that seem a little crazy. "Having the confidence to take on big challenges is so valuable," David says. "I hope we can pass that on to our kids."

Looking back, "a lot of life happened on that trip," says David. "There are so many good and bad memories, but we were certainly stretched as a family, which is what we wanted. This experience has broadened our minds. We saw so many beautiful things. We made lifelong friends. And we discovered a deeper level of empathy. I'm sure we'll continue to be inspired by this adventure for the rest of our lives."

Explore More

AMERICA'S BEST IDEA

America's National Park Service exists to preserve the country's natural and cultural resources for the inspiration of this and future generations.

PLACES FOR PEOPLE

In 1916, the U.S. National Park Service was created. Today, the NPS' 20,000 employees (and countless volunteers) safeguard America's special places and share them with more than 300 million visitors per year.

THE PARKS BY THE NUMBERS

The NPS protects over 34 million hectares (84 million acres) of wild landscapes and 407 sites, including the 62 national parks, 127 historical sites, 78 monuments, 25 military parks, and 28,968 kilometers (18,000 miles) of hiking trails.

AMERICA'S NATURAL WONDERS

Sequoia National Park is home to the largest living tree in the world. Hawaii's Volcanoes National Park is home to the world's largest volcano. The Grand Canyon, in Arizona, is one of the Natural Wonders of the World.

INVEST IN ADVENTURE

The NPS offers an annual pass that grants families access to all 62 of America's national parks for less than $100 (€88). Arguably, this is the single best investment in adventure a family could ever make.

California Dreaming: Making a Fresh Start in America's Wild West

USA

BIRGIT AND RAUL SFAT, MILLA (11)

A European family relocates to San Francisco in search of sunshine, healing, and new adventures.

For Birgit and Raul Sfat, the plan was to relocate to San Francisco temporarily—perhaps for a year or two—before returning to Germany when it was time for their four-year-old daughter Milla to start school. But, when the entire family unexpectedly fell in love with their new life in California—with the beaches, the stunning nature, and a diverse and supportive community of friends—they decided there was no need to rush back to Europe. For the next six years, San Francisco became the base from which the Sfats made a fresh start, and grew closer in ways they never imagined possible.

The family's decision to move to California in 2013 was rooted in sorrow. Around the time Milla turned four, they experienced two heartbreaking losses: first, Birgit's father died of pancreatic cancer, and soon after, Birgit and Raul lost their second daughter in a premature birth. "We decided we needed to go somewhere else for a while," says Birgit. "All of us needed to get away and find some healing and some new perspective." The family chose San Francisco, Birgit explains, because Raul had work connections there and they liked the city's colorful history and unique diversity. "We felt inspired by the way San Francisco has long been a place that welcomed people from around the world, people looking for a new, different kind of life: people like us."

sunrader

In the spring of 2019, as the family's extended stay in America was nearing an end, the Sfats decided to make the most of their last few months in the U.S. by traveling to as many of the country's natural wonders as possible.

Looking back on their time in America, Birgit Sfat believes much of the family's positive experience was thanks to the ways their daughter helped them to open up in a new culture.

Everywhere they went in America, says Birgit Sfat, her family made new and incredible memories—memories that have helped the family to heal and given them stories they will tell for the rest of their lives.

"We felt so adventurous. The nature and wildlife was unbelievable in all the national parks we visited but Yellowstone was really special, right there at the end of our long American adventure."

For the Sfats, the transition into their new life was relatively smooth. "It was amazing how helpful most people were," Birgit says. "We loved the tolerance, open-mindedness, and creativity of the San Franciscans we met; also their engagement in political and environmental issues. There was so much willingness to try new things."

Fast-forward to the spring of 2019 and, as the family's time in America was nearing an end, they decided to make the most of their last months in the U. S. by traveling to as many of the country's natural wonders as possible. They worked together to renovate a 1984 Toyota Sunrader camper van—nicknamed "Sunny"— and set out on a round trip jaunt from San Francisco to Marfa, Texas. Along the way, the family visited five stunning national parks: Death Valley in Nevada, Monument Valley in Utah, White Sands in New Mexico, and Antelope Canyon and Grand Canyon in Arizona. Looking back on that first road trip, Birgit is still in awe of the variety of landscapes they encountered. "It is simply amazing how huge and wild America is," she recalls. "On that first evening, driving through the Sierra Nevada, we were worried because we didn't have snow chains on the van. After spending a really cold night somewhere near Mono Lake, just a few hours later we were walking the sand dunes of Death Valley and nearly sweating to death."

In each of the national parks they visited, the family came into contact with the sublime magic of nature, most unforgettably in White Sands: "We were walking among the dunes, and then the sun started to set," Birgit says. "All of a sudden, it felt like we were alone on a white planet that was glowing in orange light; it was totally magnificent, one of the most beautiful moments our family has ever experienced together."

In June 2019, the Sfats said goodbye to San Francisco, the city where they had come to seek healing six years before, and loaded up "Sunny" for one last, epic road trip. This time, the family journeyed east through the vast American heartland en route to Chicago, where they caught a plane back to Europe. On the way, they spent a few days in Yellowstone, established in 1872 as the world's first national park. Armed with bear spray, the family explored its iconic geysers, towering waterfalls, and fields of wildflowers. "We felt so adventurous," Birgit recalls. "Several times, we had to stop the van and let these massive bison cross the road in front of us; and we were told to always be on the lookout for wolves, bears, and moose. The nature and wildlife was unbelievable in all the national parks we visited but Yellowstone was really special, right there at the end of our long American adventure."

Today, the family has resettled in Portugal—although 11-year-old Milla still proudly describes herself as a "California girl." Looking back on their time in America, Birgit believes much of the family's positive experience was thanks to the ways their daughter helped them to open up in a new culture. "Milla is such a great traveler," says Birgit, "and because she is much more open than her 'very German parents,' she was always our door-opener. The best things that happened to us were because of Milla: She was the one who got us invited to join a family barbecue in a small town we visited, or who was invited to make music with the street musicians. Cowboys let her ride their horses, and the oyster farmers we met were more than happy to show her how to dig for clams."

Everywhere they went in America, says Birgit Sfat, her family made new and incredible memories—memories that have helped the family to heal and given them stories they will tell for the rest of their lives.

Explore More

THE CITY BY THE BAY
There is much for families to love about San Francisco: the climate, the giant trees, the charming cable cars, the sea, the smells, and the sights. But bring your walking shoes, the hills can be brutal.

GO ON TOUR
Although guided tours might not normally be your thing, San Francisco is a big, hilly city. So, a guided tour of one kind or another will ultimately help your family see and do more.

EXPERIENCE MUIR WOODS
Just north of SF is the magical Muir Woods, a protected woodland home to 97 hectares (240 acres) of old-growth redwood trees, most of which are 500 to 800 years old (the oldest is more than 1,200 years old).

THE KIDS ARE GONNA LOVE IT
The California Academy of Sciences, the Aquarium of the Bay, the Japanese Tea Garden in Golden Gate Park, Pier 39, and the Walt Disney Family Museum are just a few of the fun, family-friendly things to do.

AN ESSENTIAL EXPERIENCE
Riding a cable car up and down the hills of San Francisco is one touristy experience that is, in fact, well worth the hype. A ride on the Powell-Hyde line is equal parts charming, fascinating, and practical.

Driving While Under the Influence of Child

By Jessica Delfino

When we take a family road trip, it looks like we are moving house. I'm a chronic overpacker with a touch of the hoarder gene in my family, and I collect … *things*. My husband teases me for it, but he has amassed an impressive array of camping gear and tools himself, every piece of which has its own special spot in our car. Thankfully, we only have one small child, or we might need to make some hard decisions regarding who comes and who stays home.

On my insistence, we bought an official family luggage set. It is ugly, plain, and black. It consists of a large, medium, and small suitcase on wheels, and a duffel bag. I usually select the largest case and pack for my son and myself. The simple luxury of being able to pack for me and me alone is ancient history.

We live in New York City, which we love and hate in equal parts, so most weekends, we make a beeline for the country. We were fortunate enough to purchase an investment property upstate that we fell so in love with we couldn't bear renting it out to random strangers, with their habits and the invisible micromaterials they'd leave behind, to say nothing of the cootie factor. So it's now our own personal Airbnb. Without traffic, we can hear the driveway's crackling rocks under our tires in just under two hours.

I do not pack lightly. I don't even try. For my son, I bring: three pairs of shirts, pants, socks, underwear, and pajamas, the nebulizer, his sundries, toothbrush and kid toothpaste, diapers, his robe and slippers, bathing suit, swim diapers, water shoes, life jacket, boots, sneakers, a light and a heavy jacket, his gloves and hat, his bag of toys, books, the iPad and charger, children's movies, his water bottles, eating utensils, and any random last-minute items he deems must-haves—a drawing he made at school, stickers, his stuffed bunny, a Band-Aid.

For myself, I gather: three tank tops and T-shirts, long-sleeved shirts, pants, underwear, socks, a dress I won't wear, a sweater, my robe, swimsuit and flip-flops, a light and a heavy jacket, my sundries, toothbrush and adult toothpaste, hat, scarf, and gloves, my laptop, Fitbit, phone and chargers, my notebook, books I'm reading, sneakers, boots, sunglasses, backup sunglasses, reading glasses, and a variety of pens and markers.

I also prepare a thermos of hot tea, a bottle of water for my son, snacks for the ride, useful items from the kitchen, and any spotty bananas that won't make it through the weekend. This is all while wrangling a flying monkey-child who couldn't sit still if sitting smelled like candy and made a lot of beeping sounds.

Closing the suitcase is an exercise in patience and skill. All my body weight is used to flatten it squarely so I can zip it shut. Thankfully it has wheels, otherwise I'd need a neighborly bodybuilder to load it into the car for me, along with the bag of toys, case of food, tote of kitchen items, one child, my purse full of work materials, and my tea.

In complete silence and calm, my husband opens the duffel, tosses in a pair of boxers, a T-shirt and a toothbrush, running shorts and sneakers, swim trunks and flip-flops.

A few times per summer and fall, we take a longer trip four hours north to dig for quartz crystal at a tourist mine and campsite in upstate New York. We don't have access to a Cessna or a chopper, so we drive.

We've taken this drive many times. So obviously, my son is still not accustomed to it and requires constant stimulation. I feel like I'm a game-show contestant in a program called *How About This?* In this so-called game, I hand my son a toy that amuses him for anywhere from ten minutes to four seconds and then he drops it on the ground, in the best-case scenario. Worst-case scenario, it gets tossed angrily and hazardously away. The grand prize is that after he cycles through all the toys—the small box that plays childlike digital recreations of classical songs, the paint pad that makes illustrations appear as he "paints" it with a brush, the books, the keyboard that plays a series of children's songs at the push of a key, the bright thing that jingles, the odd-shaped thing that tweets, and the bevy of trains and cars—he gets to watch the iPad. I try to put it off for as long as I can. I've read the stories. I don't want to be the mom who let her child watch ten minutes too many on the device and accidentally raised a serial killer. Not on my watch.

Making up games is an iPad delay tactic. In one called *Look at That!*, I yell, "Look at that!" with wild enthusiasm when we pass something even remotely interesting, becoming a circus announcer for mundane objects. "It's a … dump truck!" I squeal. "Woah, look at that radio antenna!" I announce. Each thing buys me 11 seconds of peace, and not one second more. "Look out the window and find something … red!" I say. My son bites. After we go through all the colors twice, the game devolves to: "Just look out the window at the trees and think about what it's like to be a tree."

At least once a trip, we stop at Wawa, where one can purchase gas, all varieties of processed food, a sadly assembled sandwich, hot coffee, and use the bathroom. My son adores the poorly lit cesspool. "Wawa!" he starts chanting as soon as we pull away from our curb, and repeats himself until we are in the godforsaken parking lot. Upon arrival, we get him a tiny cup of hot chocolate, which he calls his "coffee," and I get sandwiches or snacks for us all to share. The rest of the time, I chase him around the store while he examines every aisle as though he's never been there before, collecting smiles the whole way.

At some point after the sandwich but before arriving at our destination comes the most magical moment of the trip: he falls asleep. I see the signs and begin to quietly prepare. First, he gets the far-off gaze, then the yawning starts. I busy myself in a magazine. Moments later, I notice it's been quiet in the car for over 30 seconds. And he's down. My shoulders loosen. I sigh. It's break time for mama. Could be 30 minutes, could be for the rest of the ride. It's a roll of the dice, but I'll take it.

No matter how long our trip, whether to our house or to the campsite, I cherish the quiet moments. I can write, read, and almost feel like my old self again. My husband and I can talk without fear of projectiles. It allows me to refresh and rest from my full-time job, which I sometimes wonder if I'm even cut out for, though I put in my all, like a basketball player who's excited to be on the team, though he's a little short.

Being a parent is a special skill set that I'm still honing as I go, and in the car, it is magnified; condensed and concentrated, offering a fast track to a full degree.

At this rate, in just a few summers, I'll have my PhD.

JESSICA DELFINO is a writer whose work has appeared in publications including the New Yorker, *the* New York Times, *and the* Atlantic. *She is also a comedian and cheeky musician who has appeared on the BBC, Good Morning America, Dr Demento, and festivals worldwide. She documents her family life on YouTube @SmithFamilyFolio and goofs off on Twitter and Instagram @jessicadelfino.*

Each Day More Beautiful than the Last: A Road Trip through New Zealand

NEW ZEALAND

MARTA GREBER AND MIA (2.5)

After becoming a mother, a lifelong traveler discovers the joys of sharing the journey with her young daughter.

For blogger Marta Greber, traveling has been a way of life ever since she was a kid tagging along on adventurous holidays with her parents. Years later, while traveling in South America for six months, she decided to step back from her career as a lawyer and take some time to consider the future. As Marta began thinking through what to do next and what she really wanted out of life, it became clear that traveling to new places and engaging with new cultures should be at the center of whatever came next.

"For years, my husband Tomasz and I were actively looking for the 'best' place to live in the world," Marta explains. "Tomasz and I would travel to a new country and stay for three months each year, just to try it out; we both work from home, so it was relatively easy for us." When her daughter Mia was born in 2014, she feared the adventurous chapter of her life had come to an end. "When Mia arrived, I was sure my traveling days were over," Marta says. But she soon learned that a new chapter was just beginning.

Almost from day one, the couple found that traveling with Mia was not only possible but surprisingly fun. "Mia spent a lot of time on buses, planes, and trains early on, and she seemed to love it; apparently traveling makes us both super happy." After taking a few short trips around Europe, the family ventured farther

“I accepted that this trip wasn’t going to be like my other travels and I made some changes after the first few days,” Marta says. “I reduced my work hours, refocused on having fun with Mia, and created a new routine for us.”

In order to get the most out of their days together, Marta started waking up before dawn to secure a quiet hour or two for herself each day. "I needed that time to watch the sunrise, work for a while, and prepare myself for the day ahead," she says.

"Animals have such incredible power over a child's imagination. I can't express how amazing it is to see a penguin in its natural habitat—it honestly felt like a dream."

afield, leaving their home in Berlin for a 10-day stay in Hong Kong. This adventure convinced Marta that she and Mia were ready to spread their wings wider and take their first mother-daughter "girls' trip" together: a three-week-long road trip through New Zealand, the island nation whose lush landscapes and hospitable people had first charmed Marta during a visit with friends back in 2009. "Tomasz had to travel elsewhere for work, so I decided to show Mia how beautiful New Zealand is," she explains. "This time around, I didn't plan at all: I just booked a flight, hired the van, and that was it."

After landing in Christchurch, the largest city on New Zealand's South Island, Marta picked up the camper van that would be their home on the road. As she strapped her daughter into her car seat, the reality suddenly hit her: "There I was, halfway around the world, sitting in this little yellow VW camper. Mia was getting hungry, and it was starting to get dark outside. I didn't have the internet on my phone and I wasn't sure how to get to our first destination. But, we just hit the road." Her traveler's instincts kicked in and, soon, Marta found a nice, safe spot outside of Christchurch to spend their first night in New Zealand. "In the morning, we woke up to these perfect, sweeping views at sunrise; it was a beautiful moment that felt like a marker for us: our journey had now officially started."

It took some time for Marta to establish the daily routine that would sustain mother and daughter during the weeks of driving and exploration to come. "The first three days were pretty stressful," she says. "I was trying to drive, work as much as I could, and cook all the meals—plus, I wanted to play with Mia and see new places each day." Marta realized an adjustment was needed. "I accepted that this trip wasn't going to be like my other travels and I made some changes," she says. "I reduced my work hours, refocused on having fun with Mia, and created a new routine for us." In order to get the most out of their days together, Marta started waking up before dawn to secure a quiet hour or two for herself each day. "I needed that time to watch the sunrise, work for a while, and prepare myself for the day ahead," she says. Once

The trip reinforced many of Marta's long-held philosophies: "For me, the things that make traveling great are pretty simple," she says. "Be flexible, get lots of sleep, make some time for yourself, don't plan too much, and pack light, especially when you have kids."

"The sky was so dark that it was alive with the light from countless stars. I will always remember that night. Lying there with Mia in our van looking at the sky was one of the happiest moments of my life."

Mia awoke, they would eat breakfast, play, and spend the morning exploring. While Mia napped, Marta drove. For the occasional long drives, a few episodes of *Peppa Pig* helped Mia pass the time in her car seat. "In the end, we came up with a good rhythm," Marta says. "I became very attuned to our ever-changing surroundings and to each of our needs."

Throughout their journey, the pair came into close contact with New Zealand's vast diversity of flora and fauna. At Colac Bay, they happened upon a wild horse strolling on the beach. At the base of a historic lighthouse in Otara, they observed a colony of roaring, flapping sea lions. In Papatowai, they watched as cows and sheep roamed the hillsides grazing peacefully. And in Moeraki, they discovered a rookery of penguins fishing and playing near the shore. "Animals have such incredible power over a child's imagination," Marta says. "I can't express how amazing it is to see a penguin in its natural habitat—it honestly felt like a dream."

During their three-week tour of New Zealand, Marta acquired a wealth of priceless shared memories with her daughter, and also gained new insights about both parenting and traveling. "On the road with Mia, I learned to be flexible," she explains. "I can plan something I think is amazing, and Mia may not be interested, and that's okay. I had to learn to let those plans go sometimes. I know Mia will always want to run and jump and climb, so when other plans aren't working, that's my go-to solution: just go play!" From a practical perspective, the trip also reinforced many of Marta's long-held philosophies: "For me, the things that make traveling great are pretty simple," she says. "Be flexible, get lots of sleep, make some time for yourself, don't plan too much, and pack light, especially when you have kids. Most important of all," Marta says, "you have to slow down and try to enjoy each shared moment, each simple or spectacular activity. This is a time with your child you will never get back, so enjoy it."

With each new adventure, Marta Greber reaffirms her belief in the power of travel to transform our understanding of the self and to create empathy and connection with the people we meet along the way. "I don't need things to be happy," she reflects. "Living in a camper has convinced me that having less is easier; traveling this way also allows me to meet people I never would otherwise." These are lessons that Marta hopes Mia will also embrace as she grows up: "I can see how these family travels make her curious, open-minded, tolerant, and patient. And I love seeing the impact they have on her."

Looking back, Marta has a deep fondness for the unique journey she shared with Mia in New Zealand—so much fondness in fact, that her family returned for another tour of the South Island in 2019, this time with dad along for the ride.

Explore More

THE LAND OF THE KIWIS

Famous for its unspoiled landscapes, progressive politics, and quirky cultural exports, the remote island nation of New Zealand is, without question, one of the most beautiful places on Earth.

NORTH VS. SOUTH

NZ's North Island is home to Wellington (the capital), beaches, volcanoes, and thermal baths. On the South Island, you'll encounter stunning mountains, glaciers, fjords, and epic national parks.

MEET THE MĀORI

The indigenous Māori people came to NZ from eastern Polynesia in the 14th century (via canoe!) and, over the next centuries, developed a rich, distinct culture. Tip: visit Tamaki Māori Village in Rotorua.

GETTING AROUND

New Zealand spans more than 1,600 kilometers (994 miles) from end to end. So, a car/van will give you the most freedom to pull over and take in the lush landscapes. But it's also possible to fly or take trains.

MORE THAN HOBBITON

Yes, you should definitely visit Frodo's house (the *LOTR* movies were famously filmed in NZ). But, don't forget to also go hiking, biking, skiing, surfing, and caving in the Waitomo Glowworm Caves.

New Zealand has one of the darkest skies in the world as much of the country has no light pollution. The clear skies make stargazing a breathtakingly magical experience.

Into the Great Wide Open: Dads, Kids, and the Joys of a Journey Shared

LA-based Wilderness Collective was created to help people to discover a rhythm of adventure in their lives. In 2019, they introduced a series of "Dads & Kiddos" trips inspired by the birth of founder Steve Dubbeldam's son, Judah.

STEVE AND SARAH DUBBELDAM, JUDAH (3), AARO (2 MONTHS)

Steve Dubbeldam grew up on 16 hectares (40 acres) in rural Alberta, in a place he calls, "the absolute middle of nowhere. My cousins lived on the same property, so we were always outside together, usually coming up with adventures that involved wheels, motors, and risk." As kids, Steve and his cousins would ride their dirt bikes into the forest and spend days at a time camping and exploring, happily getting lost in nature. Then, in 2004, Steve moved to Los Angeles to develop an apparel start-up venture. Soon after, he began to feel that something significant was missing in his life. "I had spent 20 years of my life actively engaged with nature, and then I moved to one of the biggest cities in the world, and I stopped doing that," he says. "I felt stuck, and I knew that I needed to find a way to bring some of that wild experience here, to where I live now."

After a long period of frustration, something clicked for Steve when he began to reconsider his family's long history of intrepid invention. "Back in the 70s, my grandpa wanted to go on a sailing voyage," Steve says, "but he didn't have money for a sailboat. So, he literally went to the dump and bought some old airplane fuselages, and then, with their own hands, his family built a seaworthy trimaran." When the boat was finished, Steve's grandpa took his kids out of school for six months so that the family could sail from Toronto to Florida and back again. "At the time, I don't think my grandpa knew that this trip would have such an impact on so many people," says Steve, "but it has definitely inspired me to see that I can have a life of adventure, regardless of where I live. I'm so grateful for the legacy that he passed down to me."

Inspired by his family's fearlessness and enduring love of nature, in 2011, Steve founded Wilderness Collective, an adventure travel company with a goal to inspire and equip people to discover a rhythm of adventure in their own lives. During their first decade of operation, the Collective has taken groups of adventure-hungry urbanites on backcountry fly-fishing and horseback rides, motorbike trips between California's national parks, dune buggy cruises of the Grand Canyon, and off-road tours through Alaska's scenic mountains. "Our motto is 'Wilderness Makes You Better,'" Steve says, "and we really believe it." Along with a skilled team of guides, filmmakers, chefs, and photographers, the trips strive to bring together some of the best things in life into one experience: "Adrenaline-filled adventure, exploration of wild spaces, incredible food, and deep, soulful conversations," Steve explains. "And yes, we really do take our guests' phones away for the weekend."

Those guests—often strangers at first—come from a wide range of backgrounds: men and women, locals and internationals, first-timers and adventure veterans.

In 2019, the company started offering a whole new experience exclusively for pairs of "dads and kiddos," an evolution that was inspired by the birth of Steve's son, Judah. "I believe part of the role of a parent is to open your kids up to the world," Steve says, "to help them find their boundaries and to push them into a courageous life while being at their side the whole time." The first "Dads & Kiddos" trip was a four-day dune buggy excursion to the Grand Canyon, designed to provide a thrilling, off-road adventure for dads and just enough speed and excitement to keep the kids on the edge of their seats. "Our dream was to make these trips like a good Pixar movie: wildly fun for the kids and way better than the parents thought it would be." One of the youngest guests to beta-test that first trip was Judah Dubbeldam, who had just turned three. "I'm not joking, he still talks about that trip at least once a week," says Steve, "he wants to look at the photos and video all the time."

These specialty trips have become one of Wilderness Collective's most popular offerings. "It's an opportunity for these dads to be fully present, to feel the power of shared experience, and to do it all alongside other like-minded parents. Then, when you add kids into the mix, it just supercharges everything."

"There's no secret formula for creating adventure with your kids, but here's a good place to start: don't overthink it, ditch the devices, go somewhere that you've never been before, and don't worry about having everything figured out ahead of time."

The first "Dads & Kiddos" trip was a four-day dune buggy excursion to the Grand Canyon, designed to provide a thrilling, off-road adventure for dads and just enough speed and excitement to keep the kids on the edge of their seats.

Wilderness Collective's guided trips strive to bring together some of the best things in life into one experience: "adrenaline-filled adventure, exploration of wild spaces, incredible food, and deep, soulful conversations."

An especially powerful element of the Wilderness Collective experience is the chance for a little digital detox. "We've been taking phones away from day one," Steve explains, "which can be a shock to folk's systems; it forces them to reset their addiction to distraction and helps people to actually be in the moment instead of trying to capture themselves 'being in the moment.'" By day four of each trip, nobody is reaching for their phone anymore. "These trips help guests to get their focus back, and then suddenly, this new space opens up for deeper experience and true introspection," Steve says. After one such journey, a young girl wrote to say that her favorite thing about the trip was that no phones were allowed. "Translation," Steve explains, "she had her dad's undivided attention for four entire days."

After a decade of leading device-free, anything-can-happen journeys into the wild, the team continues to dream up new experiences. Currently in the works is a program of "Family Trips," and the very real possibility of some mother-daughter adventures before too long.

But whether or not families join a Wilderness Collective experience or not, Steve says, there are endless possibilities for moms and dads to create adventure in their everyday lives. "There's no secret formula for creating adventure with your kids," he says, "but here's a good place to start: don't overthink it, ditch the devices, go somewhere that you've never been before, and don't worry about having everything figured out ahead of time. Experience is far more powerful when both kids and parents are activating their 'learner brains.' The whole point is shared experience and undistracted time together, not having the best gear or the most epic photos to post online. Anyway," he adds, "it's always good to remember the wise words of Yvon Chouinard: 'It's not an adventure until something goes wrong.'"

"Experience is far more powerful when both kids and parents are activating their 'learner brains.' The whole point is shared experience and undistracted time together, not having the best gear or the most epic photos to post online."

"We've been taking phones away from day one," says Steve Dubbeldam, "which forces folk's to reset their addiction to distraction and helps people to actually be in the moment instead of trying to capture themselves 'being in the moment.'"

“Adventure provides an ideal context for personal growth. It involves being disconnected from day-to-day life, trying something new, being with people you care about, and accepting and managing risk.”

Our Forever Place: Discovering Home during a Journey around the World

BYRON BAY, AUSTRALIA

COURTNEY AND MICHAEL ADAMO, EASTON (15), QUIN (13), IVY (11), MARLOW (7), AND WILKIE (3)

Ready for a slower way of life, a family sells everything and circles the globe in search of a new place to call home.

Home. There may be no more powerful word in the English language. It is both a place and an idea, as big as nations and as intimate as the smell of supper on the stove. For many families, this vision is tangible—a house down the street or the city by the sea. But for others, unlocking a new dream of home requires a journey into the unknown. For Courtney and Michael Adamo, it would take an 18-month, round-the-world adventure to help them uncover the place they would ultimately call home.

In 2015, after living and working in London for more than a decade, Courtney and Michael—both of whom are American born—felt it was time for their family to make a change. So, they came up with a plan: sell everything, leave London indefinitely, and circumnavigate the globe with their four children on a "family gap year." Although the idea was something Courtney had dreamed of doing for years, the adventure had a unique dimension: "We truly hoped this year of traveling the world would inspire all of us," Courtney says, "and, along the way, we also hoped to discover a new place we could call home." After careful calculations, the Adamos knew they would be able to afford a year, more or less, of budget-savvy travel. And so, in November of 2015, the family of six left England behind and set off to see the world.

Located on Australia's east coast, Byron Bay is an idyllic resort town and surfers' paradise known for its scenic headland, pristine beaches, and a laid-back, bohemian culture that attracts dreamers looking for a simpler, more sun-kissed way of life.

"By the time we got to Byron Bay, we'd already been traveling for seven months," says Courtney Adamo, "and we had visited other places that ticked a lot of boxes for us, but it really wasn't until we got here that we all felt sure this was 'our place.'"

"Back in London," says Courtney Adamo, "we tried to spend as much time in nature as possible, but here, we literally live our lives outside. Our doors and windows are always open, the kids are constantly running in and out of the house, playing in the backyard."

Over the next year and a half, the Adamos traveled to the United States, to Mexico, South America, throughout Europe, to Sri Lanka, Japan, and Australia. Courtney documented her family's travels via Instagram and on her blog, *Somewhere Slower,* where she shared highlights from surfing in Sri Lanka to basket weaving in Brazil and slurping up soba in Kyoto. "Our family learned so much," Courtney says. "We made so many priceless memories, met wonderful new friends everywhere we went, and gained such a valuable new perspective on the world; it was an education for each of us."

On the road, the Adamos also developed a deeper appreciation for life's simple pleasures. Ultimately, these were lessons that helped shape their vision for both the kind of place they would settle down in and the life they would lead there. "We learned how little we actually need to be happy," Courtney explains. "We each spent more than a year living out of a small suitcase, wearing the same few outfits on rotation, sleeping in rented beds with just a few personal possessions to hand, and yet none of us missed the things we left behind. It wasn't easy to part with all the things we thought we needed, but it was very liberating once we did. I hope we can always be reminded of those simple, happy days." But, of all the inspiring experiences the Adamos had, none made a more powerful impression than the time they spent in a small Aussie surf town called Byron Bay.

Located on Australia's east coast, between Brisbane and Sydney, Byron Bay is an idyllic resort town and surfers' paradise known for its scenic headland, pristine beaches, and laid-back, bohemian culture. In recent years, this little town has become something of a gathering place for social-media savvy dreamers and entrepreneurs looking for a simpler, more sun-kissed way of life. "We were struck by how green and lush it is here," Courtney recalls. "You have stunning beaches and some of the world's best surf breaks, but you also have the beautiful 'hinterland' with waterfalls, secret swimming holes, and warm tea tree lakes."

Yet what stood out most to the Adamos was Byron Bay's tangible sense of community. "Right away, it struck us how much we had in common with the people we met here," Courtney says, "a genuine, shared connection with regards to what is most important in life: family time, being outdoors, good food and coffee, protecting the environment, and supporting local businesses." Everywhere they went in Byron Bay, Courtney recalls, they encountered friendly, creative, like-minded families. "We were really impressed with the simplicity of life here: no fancy cars, no enormous houses, no rush, no big queues. People here work to live. We felt very much at home amongst these happy hippies. It took us about four days to announce that we wanted to live here; we were driving in the car and I remember the kids squealing with excitement in the back seat."

The Adamos moved to Byron Bay in November 2016 and have no plans to leave anytime soon. "There is a road we drive down from our house to the beach, and every single time we do that drive, I have this pinch-me moment of how lucky we are to be here," says Courtney. "I've never lived somewhere and felt like it was my forever place—not until we moved here." As they had hoped, the family's new life in Byron Bay has allowed the Adamos to prioritize simplicity, family time, and the outdoors. "Living here in Byron has kept our kids young and free," Courtney says. "Back in London, we tried to spend as much time in nature as possible, but here, we literally live our lives outside. Our doors and windows are always open, the kids are constantly running in and out of the house, playing in the backyard. Most days, we pick them up from school and head straight to the beach. There is something so peaceful about the simplicity of our lives."

Despite the fact that the Adamos have now put down roots in their new home country—and welcomed a fifth child, Wilkie—Michael and Courtney are quick to acknowledge the continued importance of travel. "It's a blissful little bubble here in Byron, but we do lack the cultural diversity we had in London, so we'll keep venturing out to learn more about the world." Having traveled so much in their childhood, the Adamo kids already have travel dreams of their own. "All our kids are adventurous," Courtney says. "We often joke that the downside of traveling with your kids is that by introducing them to all those wonderful places and people, they will most likely scatter around the globe someday, far from home. Selfishly speaking, I hope they will always want to return home to Byron, but I do hope that each of them has some big adventures ahead of them."

Explore More

WHAT'S IN A NAME?
Byron Bay was named after the British naval officer John Byron, grandfather of the Romantic poet Lord Byron. The indigenous Arakwal people's name for the area is *Cavvanbah,* which means "meeting place."

SEE YOU AT THE BEACH
Tourists first came to Byron in the 1960s for the surf breaks and the beaches. Main, Clarkes, Wategos, Tallows, and Cosy Corner are the five beaches that attract more than two million visitors to town each year.

FOLLOW THE LIGHT
Built on the headland in 1901, the iconic Cape Byron Lighthouse was operated by resident keepers until 1989. Today, locals gather here each morning to watch the sunrise over the Pacific Ocean.

INTO THE HINTERLAND
The area around Byron Bay is replete with nature preserves. Highlights include Nightcap National Park, Minyon Falls, Broken Head, Brunswick Heads, and Protestors Falls, a unique patch of preserved rain forest.

EAT YOUR VEGGIES
The regular farmers' markets in and around Byron Bay are a big deal. It's not only a place to source quality produce, it's a chance to mingle with the locals.

Index

GONG FAMILY
PP. 192–199
yoyo-mom.com/en
Instagram: @yoyomommag
Photography by
Jaimee Gong

GREBER FAMILY
PP. 234–243
whatshouldieatforbreakfasttoday.com
Instagram: @whatforbreakfast
Photography by
Marta Greber

HERNANDEZ/SURRATT FAMILY
CAMP WANDAWEGA
PP. 204–213
wandawega.com
Instagram: @campwandawega
Photography by Julia Stotz
(204, 209, 210, 211 bottom, 213),
Jane Goodrich Photography
(205 left, 206, 208 top, 211 top),
Thayer Gowdy (205 right, 207,
208 bottom, 212)

LIVSIC FAMILY
PP. 152–161
aboutlittlej.com
Instagram: @about.little.j
Photography by
Anna Livsic

MCKAMY FAMILY
PP. 90–95
tkmckamy.com
Instagram: @tkmckamy
Photography by
Nick Onken (90, 92 top,
94 bottom right),
TK McKamy (91, 92 bottom,
93, 94 top and bottom left)

MCLEOD FAMILY
PP. 104–111
wanderingwithmary.com
Instagram: @wanderingwithmary
Photography by
Mary McLeod

METZLER-JÄGER FAMILY
PP. 38–43
maybe-you-like.com
Instagram: @maybeyoulike
Photography by
Sophia and Chris Jäger

MORENO/CHEYLUS MORENO
PP. 60–67
ilovequeencharlotte.com
Instagram: @loismoreno_
Photography by
Lois Moreno

NICHOLAS FAMILY
PP. 30–35
courtesydev.com
Instagram: @virgthebird
Photography by Rasmus
Kongsgaard (30-33, 34 top
and bottom right),
Virgil Nicholas
(34 bottom left)

OWEN FAMILY
PP. 184–191
nobackhome.com
Instagram: @nobackhome
Photography by
Karilyn Owen

PENNER FAMILY
PP. 132–141
quartiercollective.com
Instagram: @quartiercollective
Photography by
Quartier Collective

RAMU FAMILY
PP. 112–119
musuta.com
Instagram: @jopsu
Photography by
Jopsu Ramu
(112, 114–119),
Amelia Fullarton (113)

SAILSBURY FAMILY
PP. 4–7
austinsails.com
Instagram: @austinsailsbury
Photography by
Lars Hauschildt (5 top),
Austin Sailsbury
(5 bottom, 6)

SFAT FAMILY
PP. 224–231
overtheocean.com
Instagram: @overtheocean_com
Photography by
Birgit Sfat
(224, 225 bottom, 226–230),
Thayer Gowdy (225 top)

Family Adventures

Exploring the World with Children

This book was conceived, edited, and designed by gestalten.

Edited by Robert Klanten and Andrea Servert
Contributing Editor: Austin Sailsbury

Texts written by Austin Sailsbury (pp. 4–7, 22–35, 44–59, 68–85, 90–95, 112–119, 132–149, 172–183, 204–231, 234–261), Andrew Forrester (pp. 104–111) and Kevin Oberbauer (pp. 38–43, 96–101, 124–131, 234–243)

Texts edited by Austin Sailsbury (pp. 8–17, 60–67, 152–161, 166–171, 184–199)

Copy-Editing by Hannah Lack

Editorial Management by Lars Pietzschmann

Cover and design by Stefan Morgner
Layout by Johanna Posiege and Stefan Morgner

Photo Editor: Madeline Dudley-Yates

Illustrations by Dawid Ryski

Typefaces: Chap by Lauri Toikka and Florian Schick and Minion Pro by Robert Slimbach

Cover image by Birgit Sfat
Back cover image by Drew Martin

Printed by NINO Druck GmbH, Neustadt/Weinstr.
Made in Germany

Published by gestalten, Berlin 2020
ISBN 978-3-89955-865-4

For more information, and to order books, please visit www.gestalten.com

Bibliographic information published by the Deutsche Nationalbibliothek.
The Deutsche Nationalbibliothek lists this publication in the Deutsche Nationalbibliografie; detailed bibliographic data is available online at www.dnb.de

None of the content in this book was published in exchange for payment by commercial parties or designers; gestalten selected all included work based solely on its artistic merit.

This book was printed on paper certified according to the standards of the FSC®.